100 THINGS TO DO IN INDIANA BEFORE YOU DIE

Indiana State Museum

100

THINGS TO DO IN

INDIANA

BEFORE YOU

DIE

•••••••••••••••••••••••••

JAMIE WARD

Reedy Press
PO Box 5131
St. Louis, MO 63139, USA
www.reedypress.com

Library of Congress Control Number: 2022936998

ISBN: 9781681063867

Design by Jill Halpin

All photos are by the author unless otherwise noted.

Printed in the United States of America
22 23 24 25 26   5 4 3 2 1

DEDICATION

To my husband, Paul
Thank you for your support, putting up with all my travel shenanigans, humoring me through unexpected life difficulties, and loving me unconditionally. You'll forever be my favorite Instagram model and coffee date.

CONTENTS

Music and Entertainment

Sports and Recreation

Culture and History

Shopping and Fashion

Main Streets and Neighborhoods

PREFACE

Welcome to Indiana! It's the place I've called home for the majority of my life. It took me a while to appreciate everything this state has to offer. Growing up, I believed you had to travel outside the state to go on vacation or have an adventure. Like a lot of kids, I thought fun was found only in the states with oceans, Disney World, or movie stars. Little did I realize that Indiana was filled with its own wonders, amusements, stars, hidden gems, and exciting activities.

I've explored all corners of the state, yet I am constantly finding new things to do, eat, and explore. Narrowing down 100 things in Indiana was a challenge and not a task I took lightly. The list gives fair coverage to all of Indiana and includes iconic places, personal favorites, and hidden gems. It gives well-deserved recognition to things I believe everyone should do before they die. Of course, there are more things to do in Indiana that far exceed this list.

You might discover something about Indiana you didn't know existed. Or you might be challenged to try a new restaurant, such as the fine dining at Bonge's Tavern, tucked away in rural Perkinsville. The City Market in Indianapolis has hidden passageways called the Catacombs underneath its building. This list will take you through both big cities and unincorporated communities.

Show off all your adventures on social media using the hashtag #100thingsindiana. Discover more about Indiana and this list at fieldsandheels.com and @fieldsandheels on Instagram, Facebook, Twitter, LinkedIn, and TikTok.

fieldsandheels.com
@fieldsandheels
#100thingsindiana

• •

ACKNOWLEDGMENTS

Without my family, I never would have had the opportunity to discover my love for travel.

My parents: When I was a child, my parents frequently took my siblings and me on vacations to visit my family. We traveled across the country by vehicle; I didn't fly in an airplane until I was an adult. This instilled in me my love for road-tripping and family travel.

My grandparents: In their retirement, they traveled around in an RV and served as volunteers at camps. As a child I remember thinking how cramped and boring that must be. Now, as an adult, I realize the amazing opportunity they had to travel and meet people. It inspires me, and I miss them both.

My Aunt Kathy: When I graduated college, she took me on an East Coast road trip, just the two of us. It was the most fun, spontaneous, and rewarding road trip and launched my thirst for travel and history.

My husband and children: When my husband told me to pursue my passion for travel and writing, he really meant it. He's my biggest supporter. A big thanks to my husband and kids for tagging along on trips and adventures and being open to trying new activities.

The Midwest Travel Network: To this entire network of fellow travel writers who uplift, encourage, support, and offer advice. These incredibly talented individuals inspired me to turn my hobby into a profession.

Indiana visitors' bureaus and tourism agencies: Thank you for your help, hospitality, and hard work to ensure we are provided the best experiences Indiana has to offer!

Fish and chips from Payne's Restaurant

FOOD AND DRINK

1

SINK YOUR SWEET TOOTH INTO A SLICE OF SWEETNESS AT WICK'S PIES

In 2009, the sugar cream pie was officially named Indiana's state pie. But Wick's Pies in Winchester has been famous for its sugar cream pie since the 1940s. When Duane "Wick" Wickersham first opened the Rainbow Restaurant, he was making pies and delivering them out of a 1934 Buick Sedan. That's commitment. The current facility, purchased in 1961, produces more than 10,000 pies a day! I've consumed a few of those pies myself.

The demand for Mr. Wick's pies resulted in the opening of Mrs. Wick's Restaurant. Visitors can dine from a full-service menu, with breakfast served all day and 36 pies to choose from. Inside Mrs. Wick's Restaurant is a retail outlet, where you can purchase dessert and pot pies to take home.

Can't visit Winchester? Pies can be ordered online and shipped directly to your home.

100 Cherry St., Winchester, (765) 584-7437
wickspies.com

TIP

The retail outlet sells "imperfects" in its freezer section. If you don't mind a cracked crust or minor imperfection, you can grab one of the imperfect pies for a steep discount.

SUGAR CREAM PIE PARADISE

Sugar cream pies are baked daily at these popular Indiana restaurants and bakeries.

Blue Gate Restaurant & Bakery
195 N Van Buren St., Shipshewana, (260) 768-4725
thebluegate.com

Nick's Kitchen
506 N Jefferson St., Huntington, (260) 356-6618
nicksdowntown.com

Oasis Diner
405 W Main St., Plainfield, (317) 837-7777
oasisdiner.com

2

DRINK A GREEN RIVER FROM A 1900s SODA SHOP AND ICE CREAM PARLOR

AT ZAHARAKOS

Have you ever had a green river fountain soda? You might not be familiar with this popular lime-flavored soda if you aren't from the Midwest. It's best served from an old-fashioned soda fountain, like Zaharakos in downtown Columbus.

The Zaharako brothers opened this soda shop and ice cream parlor in 1900. Today, the shop still uses the original soda fountains to serve Zaharakos menu favorites. Unique museum items, such as pre-1900s marble soda fountains and syrup dispensers, line the walls. Visitors feel as though they are stepping back in time when they stop in for lunch, a drink, or an ice cream treat.

A marble and mahogany bar, 1908 self-playing pipe organ, and Tiffany lamp add a bit of elegance to the usual ice cream and soda shop experience.

329 Washington St., Columbus, (812) 378-1900
zaharakos.com

TIP

There are over 16 flavors of old-fashioned fountain sodas to try, including unique flavors such as cinnamon Coke and blue raspberry. A cinnamon Coke malt does not disappoint and tastes like Christmas.

KNOCK BACK AN OLD-FASHIONED SODA

Butt Drugs
115 E Chestnut St., Corydon, (812) 738-3272
buttdrugs.com

Hook's Drug Store Museum
(open daily during the Indiana State Fair and by appointment)
1202 E 38th St., Indianapolis, (317) 924-1503
hooksmuseum.org

Lewisville General Store
104 E Main St., Lewisville, (765) 987-7700
facebook.com/lewisville-general-store-112451873732392

South Side Soda Shop
1122 S Main St., Goshen, (574) 534-3790
southsidesodashop.com

3

EAT INSIDE AN AMISH BUGGY

AT DAS DUTCHMAN ESSENHAUS

Das Dutchman Essenhaus (known as "Essenhaus" to the locals) is located in Elkhart County, an area known for its Amish population and delicious comfort foods. Essenhaus serves home-cooked dishes in its restaurant and pies, doughnuts, and other baked goods in its bakery. You can dine from the menu or go for the popular breakfast, lunch, or dinner buffet.

If it's available, request to sit in an Amish buggy booth. It's an authentic buggy that seats up to four and offers diners a unique experience and bragging rights. You'll want to arrive early because the restaurant has only two of these booths available.

Adjacent to the restaurant is an entire village of activities, including carriage rides, mini-golf, shops, a bakery, bike rentals, a quilt garden, and more. The Essenhaus Inn & Conference Center provides overnight accommodations for those looking for a simple but comfortable place to stay.

240 US-20, Middlebury, (574) 825-9471
essenhaus.com

TIP

Try the Amish peanut butter. It is served with the rolls, and it is delicious! It can also be purchased in the gift shop and bakery.

4

CHOOSE FROM 100 DIFFERENT SHAKES AND SUNDAES

AT IVANHOE'S

There is no time for indecisiveness at Ivanhoe's! With 100 different flavors for shakes and sundaes, there is something for every palate. I have the most difficult time choosing a treat here, and the long lines prove that Ivanhoe's is a popular place to be. Check the menus out in advance to decide what you'd like to order.

Since 1965, Ivanhoe's Ice Cream & Sandwich Shoppe (formally Wiley's Drive-In) has been serving shakes, sundaes, burgers, tenderloins, salads, and more. It is also famous for its huge strawberry shortcakes, served seasonally and big enough for two.

Regulars to Ivanhoe's challenge themselves to the 100 Club. Club members are those who have tried all 100 varieties of shakes or sundaes. Check out the "100 Club" plaque in the dining room for a list of the members. Maybe you've just found yourself a new challenge.

979 S Main St., Upland, (765) 998-7261
ivanhoes.info

TIP

The portion sizes for the shakes and sundaes are generous. A size large is big enough for two to share.

BITE INTO A BURGER
AT THE HISTORIC OASIS DINER

Only a handful of historic diners remain on the National Road (US 40). One of them is the Oasis Diner in Plainfield; it is the only diner on the National Road in Indiana. It was established in 1954 but, under new ownership, the building was relocated to the National Road from its orginal location and underwent a major restoration in 2014.

The breakfast menu boasts flavorful Midwest names, such as the Indianapolis country fried breakfast and Kansas City loaded biscuits and gravy. For lunch or dinner, classics such as the Original Tenderloin and Oasis Burger are local favorites.

Wash your meal down with one of the handcrafted sodas. There are 10 flavors to choose from; my favorite is the butterscotch root beer. You can purchase a growler of soda to take home with you. End your meal with some dessert, such as a slice of pie or cake, a milkshake, or a malt.

405 W Main St., Plainfield, (317) 837-7777
oasisdiner.com

6

GET SAUCY
AT THE FIREHOUSE BBQ & BLUES

Enjoy some hickory-smoked barbeque in Richmond's oldest firehouse, the Firehouse BBQ & Blues. The firehouse was built in the 1860s. Two local firefighters purchased and renovated the building before opening for business in 2012.

The original stable for the horses that pulled the fire trucks is now a dining area. There is fire memorabilia throughout the building, as well as an original fire pole and live music every Friday and Saturday night. Gennett Records was founded in Richmond in the 1920s and recorded famous musicians such as Louis Armstrong, Nat King Cole, and Hoagy Carmichael. Richmond is the birthplace of jazz and blues.

Try all the house barbeque sauces. Tom's Mojo (named after the owner, Tom Broyles) is similar to a grilled cheese but filled with pulled pork and mac 'n cheese; it's amazing. The Smokin' Hog and pulled pork nachos are also customer favorites.

You'll leave happy, full, and tapping your foot to the tunes of Firehouse blues.

400 N 8th St., Richmond, (765) 488-0312
firehousebbqandblues.com

TIP

The Firehouse BBQ & Blues is nestled in Richmond, Indiana's Historic Depot District, which is rich in history, events, and things to do.

7

INDULGE IN CANDY NOSTALGIA
AT SCHIMPFF'S CONFECTIONERY

Every day Schimpff's Confectionery is whipping up batches of its homemade hard candies and chocolates, including its famous Cinnamon Red Hots, a Schimpff's original.

In operation since 1858, it is one of the oldest continuously operated family-owned candy businesses in the country. Live candy-making demonstrations are regularly available, and this is the best part of visiting Schimpff's. You can even try samples of the freshly made candy.

A small Candy Museum, with thousands of pieces of memorabilia on display, is located at the back of the building.

Schimpff's old-fashioned soda fountain offers milkshakes, malts, sundaes, and sodas. The chocolate Coke is a great choice. Lunch is served daily with diner classics such as sandwiches, soups, and homemade desserts.

347 Spring St., Jeffersonville, (812) 283-8367
schimpffs.com

INDIANA CANDY TRAIL

Abbott's Candies
48 E Walnut St., Hagerstown, (877) 801-1200
abbottscandy.com

Albanese Candy
5441 E Lincoln Hwy., Merrillville, (219) 947-3070
albanesecandy.com

DeBrand Fine Chocolates
10105 Auburn Park Dr., Fort Wayne, (260) 969-8333
debrand.com

Good's Candies
116 S Main St., Kennard, (765) 785-6776
goodscandies.com

Martinsville Candy Kitchen
46 N Main St., Martinsville, (765) 342-6390
facebook.com/martinsvillecandykitchen

Olympia Candy Kitchen
136 N Main St., Goshen, (574) 533-5040
olympiacandykitchen.com

Santa's Candy Castle
15499 N State Rd. 245, Santa Claus, (800) 356-1935
santascandycastle.com

South Bend Chocolate Company
3300 W Sample St., South Bend, (800) 301-4961
sbchocolate.com

8

BRUNCH AND LUNCH
AT CREIGHTON'S CRAZY EGG CAFÉ & COFFEE BAR

Farm-to-table freshness is guaranteed at Creighton's Crazy Egg Café, which is located on a farm. The Creightons have a thriving agribusiness with over 10,000 acres and more than three million egg-laying hens in Kosciusko County. In 2015 they opened Creighton's, using their farm products to create a unique breakfast and lunch menu.

A cozy fireplace greets guests. The café is filled with farm decor and modern country charm. The walls are accented with barn siding, the lighting fixtures are made with egg baskets, and a delightful gift shop invites you to stay a little longer.

Extraordinary dishes like the Crazy Egg Waffich and the Eggs & Bacon Benedict, smothered in the signature bacon gravy, are breakfast and brunch favorites. The Bacon Egg & Cheese Burger and Colossal Grilled Cheese are great for lunch.

You won't want to skip the coffee; the restaurant has a full-service espresso bar with more than twenty flavors of syrup to choose from. Order drinks with your meal or to go.

4217 W Old Rd. 30, Warsaw, (574) 267-3549
crazyegg.info

TIP

There are plenty of gluten-free options available on Creighton's menu.

9

TASTE THE ORIGINAL TENDERLOIN
AT NICK'S KITCHEN

The breaded pork tenderloin is a staple in Indiana. However, there is only one place where you can get the original tenderloin. Nick Freienstein opened Nick's Kitchen in 1908. It was here he created the world's first-ever breaded pork tenderloin. The same recipe is used today.

You'll want to arrive at Nick's hungry: the Original Breaded Tenderloin Sandwich is as big as the plate! Of course, you can always opt for the mini version if you aren't up to the challenge. Nick's Kitchen may not be a fancy restaurant, but it has one of the best-tasting tenderloins in Indiana. Save room for Nick's famous homemade pies; they are next in line to show off on the menu. With so many options to choose from, I suggest trying the pie flight, consisting of three half slices of your choice.

506 N Jefferson St., Huntington, (260) 356-6618
nicksdowntown.com

TIP

The Indiana Foodways Alliance has created the Tenderloin Lovers Trail, making it easy and convenient to locate restaurants serving the delicious pork sandwich that Hoosiers know and love. Check out the trail for more than 70 locations. indianafoodwaysalliance.com

10

SAVOR THE FINEST BEEF
AT JOSEPH DECUIS

Wagyu beef is the cream of the crop when it comes to meat. It's considered the world's finest beef. Wagyu refers to a class of cattle from Japan that are raised in all-natural, stress-free environments and fed special diets. I refer to them as spoiled cows. Joseph Decuis is the only restaurant in the United States raising its Wagyu beef to traditional Japanese standards.

Joseph Decuis Restaurant has been voted Indiana's #1 restaurant by OpenTable diners. This fine-dining option is impressive for a date night, special occasion, or simply a night out in the small town of Roanoke. There are six special rooms to choose from, and you need to make reservations in advance.

For a more casual dining option, the Joseph Decuis Emporium serves lunch six days a week. The menu rotates monthly but includes burgers, sandwiches, soups, and entrees with Wagyu options.

191 N Main St., Roanoke, (260) 672-1715
josephdecuis.com

Joseph Decuis offers private tours of the farm by appointment only. It has overnight accommodations available at two inns: the Inn at Joseph Decuis and the Joseph Decuis Farmstead Inn.

TRY THE "WORLD'S SPICIEST FOOD" AT ST. ELMO STEAK HOUSE

Forbes has rated St. Elmo Steak House one of the "Top 10 Classic Restaurants Worth Visiting" in the world. And for good reason; the iconic restaurant has been serving residents and visitors the best steaks in Indianapolis since 1902. Indy 500 legends, celebrities, politicians, and famous athletes have dined here.

In addition to its nationally known steaks, the restaurant has won awards for its 20,000-bottle wine cellar. That's an impressive wine cellar!

The world-famous shrimp cocktail is the only starter option on the menu. The Travel Channel classified it as the "world's spiciest food." And yes, it is quite spicy! It is served with four jumbo shrimp and the signature spicy cocktail sauce. Are you up for the challenge? Reservations are recommended.

127 S Illinois St., Indianapolis, (317) 635-0636
stelmos.com

For a more casual dining option, try the 1933 Lounge by St. Elmo. It is located on the second floor above St. Elmo and is a speakeasy-style lounge serving cocktails and bar bites, including the famous shrimp cocktail.

EXPERIENCE FARM-TO-FORK DINING
AT FAIR OAKS FARMS

You can enjoy a true farm-to-table experience at the Farmhouse Restaurant at Fair Oaks Farms in northwest Indiana. It is the #1 agritourism destination in the Midwest. In addition to the Farmhouse Restaurant, the farm has a campus of activities including museums, tours, a hotel, a café, a gift shop, a nature trail, and a dog park. Dishes at the Farmhouse are created with products grown on the farm and at other farms in the region. Trust me when I say you'll want to save room for dessert; the cake slices are big enough to feed two. The culinary team prepares everything before your eyes; a see-through wall is the only thing that separates the diners from the kitchen.

You can extend your visit with the dairy, pig, and crop tours and adventures, as well as snacks at the Cowfé and Dairycatessen. Wrap it up with a stay at the hotel, Fairfield Inn by Marriott.

856 N 600 E, Fair Oaks, (877) 536-1194
fofarms.com

TIP

Check out the Fair Oaks Farms seasonal activities and events for unique experiences.

13

SIP, CHEW, AND TOUR
AT HARD TRUTH DISTILLING COMPANY

You can spend an entire day at the Hard Truth Distilling campus in Nashville, Indiana. It's nestled on 325 wooded acres and features a distillery, rack house, smokehouse, outdoor stage, restaurant, festival grounds, walking trails, a pond, a cabin, and more. The Restaurant at Hard Truth serves American gastropub fare, local Quaff ON! beer, and a craft drink menu with Hard Truth spirits. The food is phenomenal, and the desserts are worth a splurge; they are often infused with Hard Truth spirits. Just outside the restaurant, the Hard Truth on the Rocks terrace enables guests to dine outdoors during the warmer months.

Tastings, tours, and classes are all offered on the campus as part of the experience. Engage in a single barrel selection experience, distillery tour, or mixology class, or take an ATV tour around the campus with stops and tastings.

418 Old State Rd. 46, Nashville, (812) 720-4840
hardtruthdistilling.com

TIP

The Big Woods restaurants are part of the Hard Truth family. You can visit the original Big Woods Restaurant and Big Woods Pizza in Nashville, Indiana.

ENJOY FINE DINING IN AN UNUSUAL LOCATION

AT BONGE'S TAVERN

You will find a mix of class and quirkiness at Bonge's Tavern in Perkinsville, a town with a population of less than 120. Bonge's Tavern isn't your standard fine-dining establishment; it's uniquely Indiana. It serves fresh, local food in a historic diner in the middle of rural Indiana. It has a limited menu with a selection of delicious, quality dishes such as lamb chops, filets, fish, and duck. You'll need to be 21 and older to visit, but you won't need to get dressed up. The atmosphere is relaxed and casual. In the warmer months, visitors are even welcome to tailgate outside before their reservation.

Bonge's Tavern was built in 1847, but it didn't become a tavern until 1934. The tavern was restored in the 1990s, and bits of Indiana-related history were added to the building. The walls, booths, decorations, and even lamps are all from throughout the state.

9830 W 280 N, Perkinsville, (765) 734-1625
bongestavern.com

TIP

Indiana Foodways Alliance has created more than 20 Indiana Culinary Trails, with locations all over the state. These trails include local restaurants, delis, coffee shops, distilleries, steakhouses, and more. Download the Indiana Culinary Trails Passport at Visit Indiana to earn prizes when you check in at a trail location.

visitindiana.com/cuisine

15

CELEBRATE WITH CHARCUTERIE
AT GOLFO DI NAPOLI

Golfo di Napoli knows how to create a truly enjoyable and authentic Italian experience here in Indiana. The best Italian cheeses in the state are created at the Golfo di Napoli manufacturing facility in Warren. The founders, originally from Naples, opened this organic facility, complete with a restaurant, in 2019. They use only dairy sourced from Indiana farmers and provide a true farm-to-fork dining experience in the Golfo di Napoli Caffé.

All staff are trained by Italian chefs to serve authentic Italian dishes, desserts, and coffee. The menu consists of a variety of charcuterie boards, pizzas, salads, and paninis. I suggest a Nutella pizza paired with a cappuccino for dessert. Cheeses, wines, and olive oils can be purchased in the café or the online store. In the warmer months, an outdoor patio surrounded by countryside provides a beautiful atmosphere for live music and picnics. It's the perfect date night.

7916 S Warren Rd., Warren, (260) 355-5975
golfodinapolidairy.com

TIP

You can stop by Golfo di Napoli to purchase items or pick up a coffee or espresso drink to go.

VISIT AN INDIANA CREAMERY

Crystal Springs Creamery
A small family creamery in Northern Indiana with a farm shop selling cheese curds and other dairy products.
60020 Ash Rd., Osceola, (574) 535-8442
crystalspringscreamery.com

Heritage Ridge Creamery
A creamery in Amish country where you can watch cheese being made, sample the selection, and purchase cheese.
11275 W 250 N, Middlebury, (574) 825-9511
heritageridgecreamery.com

Schnabeltier
Artisan cheese factory, brewery, and winery.
491 Apache Dr., Rochester, (574) 224-3373
schnabeltier.com

Traders Point Creamery
100% grass-fed farm, creamery, restaurant, dairy barn, and farm store.
9101 Moore Rd., Zionsville, (317) 733-1700
traderspointcreamery.com

Tulip Tree Creamery
Small-batch creamery and cheese-making classes.
6330 Corporate Dr., Indianapolis, (317) 331-5469
tuliptreecreamery.com

HAVE A MEAL BY CANDLELIGHT
AT THE STORY INN

If you drive along the winding country roads of Brown County, you'll arrive at a small village. This is Story, Indiana, a tiny 19th-century village where you'll find the Story Inn restaurant, inn, and gardens. The restaurant serves gourmet, prix fixe dinners and Sunday brunch. Reservations are required for dinner.

Life feels a bit slower here. A creaking door leads to what appears to be an 1800s general store in the dining room of the inn. The tables are candlelit for dinner, which includes four courses. It's romantic and intriguing.

If you prefer a more casual dinner, step into the underground tavern for the pub menu. The tavern is much like you would expect from an 1800s basement: it's musty, dark, mysterious, and unique. It's an experience like no other. So grab a seat in this historic inn and dine on exquisite farm-to-fork food in a village that is said to be haunted.

6404 State Rd. 135, Nashville, (812) 988-2273
storyinn.com

TIP

You can stay overnight at the Story Inn. The inn is often fully booked in the fall, so make your reservations in advance.

GRAZE AND GAZE AMONG LEGENDS

AT 33 BRICK STREET

Former NBA player Larry Bird's hometown is French Lick, and that doesn't go unnoticed in this small resort town (home to the French Lick Resort). To honor his legacy, Larry Bird Boulevard is named after him, and a sculpture of Bird hangs out around a local basketball court. Most impressive is the collection of Larry Bird (a.k.a. "Larry the Legend") memorabilia at 33 Brick Street.

33 Brick Street is a family-friendly sports bar and restaurant with a few legends of its own, namely its homemade tenderloin and burgers. While waiting for your monster burger, you can browse Bird's signed jersey, trophies, rings, and more. If you ask nicely, the staff might even let you try on his jersey. There are signed jerseys from other sports legends, as well, like Emmitt Smith, Michael Jordan, Wayne Gretzky, and Magic Johnson, to name a few.

480 S Maple St., French Lick, (812) 936-3370
33brickstreet.com

18

ASCEND THE GRAND STAIRCASE OF TIPPECANOE PLACE

This historic mansion was built in 1888 by Clem Studebaker, the president of the largest wagon manufacturer in the world. Today the mansion is called Tippecanoe Place. The 19th-century, 24,000-square-foot, four-story manor is an impressive sight. It's an even more extraordinary experience to dine in. You might even witness a marriage proposal.

Forty rooms and 20 fireplaces make up the mansion, which has been revitalized into a restaurant, brewery, event venue, and escape rooms. Tippecanoe Place Restaurant is a fine-dining establishment that serves guests on the lower and main levels of the manor. The prime rib is the signature dish. Ascend the grand, hand-carved staircase to the third level to access the Studebaker Brewing Co. The brewery has a more casual atmosphere, serving hand-crafted brews and a menu with craft beer-inspired cuisine.

620 W Washington St., South Bend, (574) 234-9077
tippe.com

DINE AT RESTAURANTS IN HISTORIC MANSIONS

Agave Mansion
110 W 9th St., Michigan City, (219) 243-7136
agavemansion.com

Fowler House Kitchen
909 South St., Lafayette, (765) 400-2002
fowlerhouse.org

Hostess House
723 W 4th St., Marion, (765) 664-3755
hostesshouse.org

The Neely House
617 E Adams St., Muncie, (765) 216-1647
theneelyhouse.com

19

NOURISH YOURSELF ALL DAY

AT FARM BLOOMINGTON

If you are looking for breakfast, lunch, dinner, or a late-night drink, the FARM restaurant in Bloomington has all these options. It offers casual, farm-to-table dining upstairs during the day, and music, trivia, and drinks downstairs at night in its Root Cellar. Owner and chef Daniel Orr opened FARM in 2008 with an emphasis on creating a menu using "local ingredients with global flavors." The restaurant is housed in a former Odd Fellows building and was restored using as much of the space to maintain the history of downtown Bloomington as possible. For a food and history lover, it's the perfect combination.

The garlic fries and buttermilk biscuits are highly recommended signature items at FARM. Herbs are grown by FARM; chefs make the condiments in-house and source produce from local farmers. It's a fresh food experience.

108 E Kirkwood Ave., Bloomington, (812) 323-0002
farm-bloomington.com

20

GRAB A (COFFEE) FLIGHT IN AN AIRPORT TERMINAL

AT CORSAIR CAFÉ

I bet you didn't expect to find an airport café in this book, but the Corsair Café isn't your typical airport coffee stand! It's a restaurant and coffee bar located inside the Terre Haute Regional Airport terminal. The terminal is open to the public and welcomes guests to the Corsair Café for coffee, breakfast, lunch, or to visit the Pilot Shop for merchandise and gifts. The restaurant is aviation-themed, has chairs with propellers for legs and menu items like the F-16 Falcon Fries and Warthog Tenderloin.

The large café windows overlook the runways, so you get a great view of the planes coming and going while you dine or sip on cold brews. Whatever you order, don't leave without getting a Coffee Flight or Fizzy Fuel Flight. It's the only place in the state where you can enjoy a flight by taste and sight at the same time.

581 S Airport St., Terre Haute, (812) 730-4887
thecorsaircafe.com

TIP

Blackerby's Hangar 5 Restaurant in Columbus is another great spot to grab breakfast or lunch. It is located inside the Columbus Municipal Airport. Visit the Atterbury-Bakalar Air Museum next door, both celebrate the history of Bakalar Air Force Base.

Blackerby's Hangar 5 Restaurant

4770 Ray Boll Blvd., Columbus, (812) 378-4010

blackerbyshangar5.com

Atterbury-Bakalar Air Museum

4742 Ray Boll Blvd, Columbus, (812) 372-4356

atterburybakalarairmuseum.org

ENJOY A FLIGHT OF COFFEE FROM A LOCAL CAFÉ

Best Friends Coffee & Bagels
1060 E Main St., Brownsburg, (317) 350-2185
facebook.com/best-friends-coffee-bagels-1595040293916074

Bizy Dips Bakery & Coffee Shop
101 S Meridian St., Portland
bizydips.com

Black Wax Café
910 N Washington St., Kokomo, (765) 457-3373
blackwaxcafe.com

The Grind Coffee House
1308 S Randolph St., Garrett, (260) 553-4283
facebook.com/garrettdrinkscoffee

The Java Bean Café
151 N 2nd St., Decatur, (260) 728-4000
thejavabeancafe.net

Latte Lounge
108 N Buffalo St., Warsaw, (574) 268-1616
lattelounge.net

The Perk Coffee House (located in Central Ministries)
5801 Schwartz Rd., Fort Wayne, (419) 487-3550
facebook.com/theperkfw

Rose & Lois
7249 E 146th St., #110, Carmel, (317) 597-5118
roseandlois.com

Well Grounded Café
14517 Lima Rd., Fort Wayne, (260) 637-6622
wellgroundedcafe.com

21

THROW BACK A FROSTY ROOT BEER

AT THE TRIPLE XXX FAMILY RESTAURANT

Guy Fieri featured Triple XXX on his *Diners, Drive-Ins and Dives* in 2007, but this family diner was making a name for itself long before that. Triple XXX started as a root beer stand in 1929, then it became Indiana's first drive-in, and today it's a family restaurant. Look for the iconic orange and black striped building on a hilltop near the Purdue University campus. The restaurant will be serving up its famous homemade root beer, breakfast special, and tenderloin. I love the sweet potato fries and sweet dipping sauce.

The restaurant is always busy, as it's a favorite among locals, students, and tourists. Indoor seating is limited to counter-style barstools and is crowded. You can't order wrong with the breakfast, burgers, or tenderloin as long as you get the frosty root beer to go with it.

2 N Salisbury St., West Lafayette, (765) 743-5373
triplexxxfamilyrestaurant.com

DRIVE-INS WITH HOMEMADE ROOT BEER

Carlson's Drive-In
118 W Coolspring Ave., Michigan City, (219) 872-0331
carlsonsdrivein.com

Dog n Suds
601 Sagamore Pkwy. S, Lafayette, (855) 364-6783
dognsudsgreaterlafayette.com

Gene's Root Beer and Hot Dogs
640 S Scatterfield Rd., Anderson, (765) 642-5768
facebook.com/genesrootbeer

Mason's Root Beer Drive-In
1201 E National Hwy., Washington, (812) 254-2830
facebook.com/pages/masons-root-beer-drive-in/111122585589201

Mug n Bun
5211 W 10th St., Indianapolis, (317) 244-5669
mug-n-bun.com

The Port Drive-In
419 N Calumet Rd., Chesterton, (219) 926-3500
theportdrivein.net

Simonton Lake Drive-In
3724 Cassopolis St., Elkhart, (574) 264-6726
simontonlakedrivein.com

DEVOUR DESSERT IN A QUIET OASIS
AT BATAR

Batar is a café, bakery, and shop surrounded by the Muscatatuck National Wildlife Refuge in southern Indiana. From the outside, Batar looks like a rustic retreat with gardens, benches, and paths. But inside is a bright, delightful dining room adorned with lattice ceilings, teapots, hanging flowers, and checkered tablecloths. It feels a bit like going to grandma's house. Lunch, dessert, and 25 flavors of tea are served on vintage china.

Batar is open seasonally, from March to December. There is one rule it strictly enforces: no cell phone conversations are allowed. Its goal is to offer guests a place to rest and relax. It's quiet in the café, except for the chatter of guests. It's not the type of place to go for a rushed lunch; instead, it invites you to stay for a while. Enjoy your dining in peace, visit the shop and gardens afterward, and always order dessert. The cookie boxes and cakes are a work of art.

12649 US-50, Seymour, (812) 522-8617
cafebatar.blogspot.com

Seymour is the birthplace of singer John Mellencamp. Check out the large mural of Mellencamp on the side of This Old Guitar Music Store.

106 W 2nd St., Seymour, (812) 524-8986
this-old-guitar-music-store.business.site

23

FANCY SOME FISH AND CHIPS
AT PAYNE'S RESTAURANT

Take a ride down (or up) Interstate 69 for some of the best fish and chips in the state. Or maybe in the entire Midwest. Payne's is an authentic British restaurant in Central Indiana, started by owner Stephen Payne in 2005. Payne is a native of Yorkshire in northern England and brings family recipes to the menu. All ingredients are locally sourced, as much as possible. The garden beds surrounding the restaurant offer fresh accompaniments to dishes.

Payne's signature fish and chips bring in diners from states away! The restaurant has North Atlantic cod freshly delivered and prepared in-house. You must get the ooey-gooey sticky toffee pudding for dessert; it's a crowd-pleaser. If the food isn't enticing enough, the quirky, vintage, and rustic restaurant design should be.

4925 S Kay Bee Dr., Gas City, (765) 998-0668
paynes-restaurant.business.site

TIP

A British Garfield statue sits in front of Payne's Restaurant. This is one of over 14 statues on Grant County's Garfield Trail, honoring the hometown of creator Jim Davis. Find more than a dozen Garfield statues on neighboring Delaware County's Garfield Trail as well.

showmegrantcounty.com/experiences/garfield
visitmuncie.org/garfield-trail-delaware-county

The Historic Artcraft Theatre

MUSIC AND ENTERTAINMENT

PICK AND GRIN INSIDE THE COUNTRY'S LARGEST MUSIC STORE

AT SWEETWATER

Even non-musicians enjoy visiting Sweetwater in Fort Wayne. It's much more than the United States' largest retail music store; it's an entire campus of amenities. Demo studios enable guests to try out instruments before they buy, or take lessons at the Sweetwater Academy of Music & Technology.

A performance stage and pavilion offer events, concerts, and jam sessions throughout the year. There are even recording studios, the Crescendo Coffee café, a diner, an arcade and game area with virtual golf, and a giant slide for kids. You can spend an entire day at Sweetwater, especially if you take in a concert. My entire family finds enjoyable things to do on the Sweetwater campus.

5501 US-30 W, Fort Wayne, (800) 222-4700
sweetwater.com

TIP

Also visit Sight & Sound Music Center in Muncie, with over 1,000 guitars on display. 4341 W Williamsburg Blvd., Muncie, (765) 289-8526 sightandsoundmusic.com

WATCH A CLASSIC FILM
AT THE HISTORIC ARTCRAFT THEATRE

Classic movies play at the Historic Artcraft Theatre every Friday and Saturday. The theater is one of the most intact art deco theaters left in the state and is on the Indiana Register of Historic Sites and Structures. It was built in 1922 as a silent movie theater but went through a renovation in 1948 to become an art deco movie house.

Expect different when you attend a show at the nonprofit Artcraft; it's a bit like stepping back into finer times. A pre-show live skit, stage banter, the traditional national anthem reel, and a classic cartoon accompany each evening movie. Matinees include a short curtain speech, the national anthem reel, and a classic cartoon. It's a different kind of movie experience, one that everyone should enjoy.

Purchase tickets online or at the box office.

57 N Main St., Franklin, (317) 736-6823
historicartcrafttheatre.org

TIP

Grab popcorn at the concession stand. Its popcorn is locally grown and has unlimited refills. Yum!

HEIGHTEN YOUR SENSES
AT THE INDIANA STATE FAIR

The Indiana State Fair entertains fairgoers with events and concerts for three weeks each July and August. The Hoosier Lottery Grandstand is located on the one-mile track and seats over 13,000. This is where all the superstars perform. A permanent stage is used to host concerts, while the track serves as a venue for spectator sporting events.

For those looking for some edgy entertainment, a demolition derby and rodeo are family-friendly, adrenaline-rush events. Celebration Park is another stage that often has free concerts. I like the less crowded, open spaces of this stage area. While visiting, take a ride on the towering Skyride. At 35 feet in the air, you'll travel above Main Street for a full view of the fairgrounds. You'll also want to try the "Taste of the Fair," an annual line-up of new, unique fair foods from a variety of concession stands.

1202 E 38th St., Indianapolis, (317) 927-7500
indianastatefair.com

DID YOU KNOW?

The largest Indiana county fair is the Elkhart County 4-H Fair, located in northern Indiana. It hosts more than 200,000 guests during a nine-day opening every July. 17746 County Rd. 34, Goshen, (574) 533-3247
4hfair.org

GET ARTSY
AT THE BOB ROSS EXPERIENCE

Minnetrista Museum and Gardens is a year-round campus featuring a museum, historic homes, gardens, play areas, and a nature area. In one of the historic homes is a permanent exhibit called the Bob Ross Experience. And it's not just any historic home; it's where Bob Ross's The Joy of Painting was filmed.

Step back into Ross's studio, a 1980s delight just the way I remember it as a kid. There is also a gallery of Ross's original artwork and a painting workshop. Tickets to the Bob Ross Experience include admission to the Minnetrista Museum and Gardens. Explore the entire 40-acre campus while you are there, and stop by the Orchard Shop to purchase exclusive Bob Ross merchandise and local goods.

1200 N Minnetrista Pkwy., Muncie, (765) 282-4848
minnetrista.net

TIP

If you're feeling hungry, Elm Street Brewing Co. makes a mean burger and tenderloin. It is featured on the Indiana Foodways Alliance's Tenderloin Lovers Trail. 519 N Elm St., Muncie, (765) 273-2054
elmstbrewing.com

BE ALL EARS FOR A CLASSIC

WITH THE INDIANAPOLIS SYMPHONY ORCHESTRA

For 40 years, the Indianapolis Symphony Orchestra has been hosting an event called Symphony on the Prairie. This outdoor music series takes place every summer weekend at Conner Prairie in Fishers. The Conner Prairie Symphony Bowl is a beautiful backdrop for concerts, as concertgoers have a view of the sunset as the orchestra plays into the evening. It's magical. A variety of genres and generations of music are represented throughout the summer, so there is something for everyone.

Symphony on the Prairie is a family-friendly event. Bring your favorite snacks and drinks for a picnic. Food vendors and concessions are also available.

13400 Allisonville Rd., Fishers, (317) 639-4300
indianapolissymphony.org

TIP

Mark your calendar for the Indiana Yuletide Celebration, held every December at the Hilbert Circle Theatre. It's been a Hoosier holiday tradition (and party) for over 30 years.

TUNE IN TO SOME LIVE MUSIC AT THE RATHSKELLER

If you enjoy live music and authentic German cuisine, you're in for a real treat at the Rathskeller. It has been named Indianapolis's #1 German restaurant, but it's also one of the top live music spots in Central Indiana. It has live music year-round, with full band shows in its Grand Kellersaal Ballroom and acoustic shows at the Kellerbar. The outdoor Biergarten is open in the summer months and hosts live entertainment under a large band shell.

The Rathskeller is located in the Athenaeum, a National Historic Landmark built in 1897 as a social club for the large community of German immigrants in Indianapolis. While there, dine on casual German specialties in the Kellerbar or enjoy formal dining in the Rathskeller. You'll feel as though you're walking through a quaint Bavarian inn.

401 E Michigan St., Indianapolis, (317) 636-0396
rathskeller.com

TIP

Take a free guided or self-guided tour of the Athenaeum, offered by the Athenaeum Foundation and Indiana Landmarks. athenaeumindy.org

RIDE
THE FRENCH LICK SCENIC RAILWAY

You can experience a (fake) train hold-up or take a magical ride to the North Pole on the Polar Express in French Lick, Indiana. The French Lick Scenic Railway is a historic 18-mile museum on a track that takes you on a trip back in time. Excursions and special events, like the Wild West Hold-Up, are available throughout the year. These excursions include reenactments, musical entertainment, and lively action. Avoid getting robbed by the Lost River Renegade!

You can also opt for a quieter option on a scenic train ride. Or choose a tasty trip, like the chocolate or bourbon tasting trains. Rides last just under two hours and pass through the Hoosier National Forest and Burton Tunnel, the second-longest rail tunnel in Indiana.

8594 W State Rd. 56, French Lick, (800) 748-7246
frenchlickscenicrailway.org

INDIANA SCENIC TRAIN RIDES

Fort Wayne Railroad
One of the last surviving steam locomotives in the world; seasonal excursions are available.
15808 Edgerton Rd., New Haven, (260) 493-0765
fortwaynerailroad.org

Hoosier Valley Railroad Museum
Museum with seasonal train rides.
507 Mulberry St., North Judson, (574) 896-3950
hoosiervalley.org

Nickel Plate Express
1950s Santa Fe passenger cars offer dining and special excursions.
825 Forest Park Dr., Noblesville, (317) 285-0682
nickelplateexpress.com

Ohio River Scenic Railway
Rides along the Ohio River in Southern Indiana.
333 7th St., Tell City, (812) 548-6848
ohiorivertrain.com

Spirit of Jasper
Luxury dining excursions.
201 Mill St., Jasper, (812) 482-5959
spiritofjaspertrain.com

Whitewater Valley Railroad
Special train rides from Connersville to Metamora, April to December.
455 Market St., Connersville, (765) 825-2054
whitewatervalleyrr.org

DRIVE THROUGH INDIANA'S LARGEST FESTIVAL IN PARKE COUNTY

The Parke County Covered Bridge Festival takes place annually on the second Friday in October. It is the largest festival in Indiana and one of the top fall road trips in the state. The covered bridges and foliage are a gorgeous background for a country drive.

Parke County is located on the northwest side of the state and is home to 31 historic covered bridges. Visitors often take several days to explore the 10-day festival. There are 10 festival locations, each offering food, shopping, entertainment, and demonstrations. Start your trip off in Rockville (the festival headquarters); here you can grab a festival map, check out the historical museum, explore the 1883 train depot, shop, and begin your covered bridge tour.

(765) 569-5226
coveredbridges.com/covered-bridge-festival

FEED YOUR INNER FOODIE

AT THE WEST SIDE NUT CLUB FALL FESTIVAL

Mark your calendar for one of the largest street festivals in the United States! The West Side Nut Club Fall Festival is a week-long gala that takes place every October in Evansville. This tradition has been going on for over 100 years and brings in more than 200,000 people annually. It's free to attend and hosted by the West Side Nut Club.

If you are a foodie, this is a great event for you! More than 130 food booths are set up to bring you the most unique, best fried treats and savory delights of the season. All day and night, Franklin Street is filled with activities, entertainment, rides, parades, and competitions.

The best part? All the proceeds go to charity.

nutclubfallfestival.com

DANCE IN DELIGHT
AT THE ELKHART JAZZ FESTIVAL

Elkhart, known as the "Band Instrument Capital of the World," has been showing off its jazz hands since 1988. Every June it hosts the three-day Elkhart Jazz Festival and brings in more than 100 musicians to perform on seven stages. Some of the stages are outside, and some are inside the Lerner Theatre. Tickets can be purchased online, but keep in mind that some of the stages outside are free.

The festival is a great time for all ages and offers a lively atmosphere. Downtown Elkhart is partially blocked off for concertgoers, and it's not unusual to find people dancing in the streets. Food vendors are set up to feed those who work up an appetite. Can you feel the rhythm?

The Lerner Theatre
410 S Main St., Elkhart, (574) 293-4469
elkhartjazzfestival.com

JAZZ ENTERTAINMENT THROUGHOUT INDIANA

B'Town Jazz Fest
Free annual jazz festival in Bloomington.
btownjazz.org

Club Soda
An old-school, fine-dining jazz club.
235 E Superior St., Fort Wayne, (260) 426-3442
clubsodafortwayne.com

Indy Jazz Fest
Organized annually by the Indianapolis Jazz Foundation.
(317) 966-7854
indyjazzfest.net

The Jazz Kitchen
A cozy live jazz venue and restaurant.
5377 N College Ave., Indianapolis, (317) 253-4900
thejazzkitchen.com

Valparaiso University Jazz Festival
An annual jazz festival organized by the university.
Valparaiso University Harre Union
1509 Chapel Dr., Valparaiso, (219) 464-5415
valpo.edu/union/programs/jazz-fest

Oinking Acres Farm & Rescue Sanctuary

SPORTS AND RECREATION

34

KISS THE BRICKS
AT THE INDIANAPOLIS MOTOR SPEEDWAY

The world's largest sports venue, the Indianapolis Motor Speedway (IMS) was built in 1909 with a historic 2.5-mile oval track. It's most famous for hosting the Indianapolis 500 every Memorial Day weekend. The speedway also hosts the IndyCar Series, NASCAR, and many other events. IMS can hold more spectators than any other sporting venue in the world.

In 1996, NASCAR champ Dale Jarrett kneeled to kiss the Yard of Bricks start-finish line after his Brickyard 400 win. Jarrett's team joined him to kiss the bricks and . . . boom, a tradition was formed. I've kissed the bricks, and you should too (bricks are sanitized between visitors). Visitors can take a Kiss the Bricks Tour through the Indianapolis Motor Speedway Museum. The guided tour includes a bus lap around the oval, a stop at the Yard of Bricks, and admission to the museum.

4750 W 16th St., Indianapolis, (317) 492-6784
imsmuseum.org

TIP

Lucas Oil Indianapolis Raceway Park is known for its drag strip, which is just one of its three unique tracks. This park is located seven miles west of the Indianapolis Motor Speedway. Lucas Oil hosts the biggest drag racing event in the world, the NHRA US Nationals, every Labor Day weekend.

10267 E US Hwy. 136, Indianapolis
(317) 969-8600
raceirp.com

SHOOT HOOPS ON THE COURT OF THE HICKORY HUSKERS

IN THE HOOSIER GYM

Basketball is big in Indiana. Especially in Knightstown, home to the Hoosier Gym. In 1985 the movie *Hoosiers* was partially filmed here. *Sports Illustrated* called it "one of the greatest movies of all time." Have you seen it? If not, I suggest watching the film before visiting. You'll be able to take joy in reliving some of the scenes as you take a "granny" shot on the court, walk through the underground locker room, or observe from the stands.

The gym was built in 1921 for the community school district but sat unused before the filming took place. Now it serves as a museum and rental facility, hosting games throughout the year. Tours are available six days a week with free admission for all (donations are appreciated).

355 N Washington St., Knightstown, (765) 345-2100
thehoosiergym.com

TIP

Another great destination marking Hoosier basketball history is the Indiana Basketball Hall of Fame. It is located just 20 minutes northeast of the Hoosier Gym. 1 Hall of Fame Ct., New Castle, (765) 529-1891
hoopshall.com

ICONIC INDIANA FIELDHOUSES

Gainbridge Fieldhouse
Home to the Indiana Pacers and Indiana Fever.
125 S Pennsylvania St., Indianapolis, (317) 917-2727
gainbridgefieldhouse.com

Hinkle Fieldhouse
Home to the Butler Bulldogs, filming site for the movie *Hoosiers*, and a National Historic Landmark.
Butler University, 510 W 49th St., Indianapolis
(317) 940-8000, butlersports.com

Mackey Arena
Home to the Purdue University Boilermakers.
900 John R. Wooden Dr., West Lafayette, (800) 497-7678
purduesports.com/facilities/mackey-arena/2

New Castle Fieldhouse
The world's largest high school fieldhouse.
801 Parkview Dr., New Castle, (765) 593-6685

Simon Skjodt Assembly Hall
Home to the Indiana University Hoosiers.
1001 E 17th St., Bloomington, (812) 855-4848
iuhoosiers.com

WATCH THE INDIANAPOLIS COLTS IN ACTION

AT LUCAS OIL STADIUM

Lucas Oil Stadium is home to the Indianapolis Colts and is quite an impressive structure. The stadium opened in 2008 and has a unique roof made up of two retractable panels, which can be opened in only 11 minutes. Each panel weighs 2.5 million pounds. Whoa!

Lucas Oil seats over 70,000 when fully expanded. With a convenient downtown location and underground pedestrian walkways, visitors can walk to the Convention Center, hotels, and the Circle Centre mall without ever going outside. Grab some tickets to a Colts game to watch them play on their home field. If you can't make it to a Colts game, 75-minute guided tours of the stadium are available on select dates. The tours are just as special as attending a game!

500 S Capitol Ave., Indianapolis, (317) 262-8600
lucasoilstadium.com

TIP

The Colts Training Camp takes place every summer and is a great way to see the players in action. It is free and open to the public. Dates and locations vary, so check the website for details. colts.com

DARE TO DO THE 3 DUNE CHALLENGE
AT INDIANA DUNES NATIONAL PARK

Along the Lake Michigan shoreline of Northwest Indiana are over 50 miles of trails in Indiana Dunes National Park. These trails offer scenic views of dunes, wetlands, prairies, rivers, forestry, and Lake Michigan. The lakeshore and endless miles of sand mounds are relaxing to the eyes, but exhausting to the body.

The 3 Dune Challenge is an adventure for those willing to work up a sweat and encounter the intimidating (but beautiful) dunes. This is one of Indiana's toughest physical challenges. Although the course is only 1.5 miles in length, it's the 552 vertical feet of climbing sand and stairs that are a challenge. The dunes are spectacular but can be dangerous to climb, so please stay on the trails.

The rewards are worth it, though—the feeling of victory and the bragging rights.

1215 State Rd. 49, Porter, (219) 395-1882
nps.gov/indu/index.htm

TIP

Start with a stop at the Indiana Dunes Visitor Center for a map, brochures, and orientation videos. Rangers are on hand to answer any questions.

38

ADMIRE INDIANA'S LARGEST WATERFALL
AT CATARACT FALLS

Cataract Falls is located on Mill Creek, which feeds into Cagles Mill Lake (also known as the Lieber and Cataract Falls State Recreation Area). There are two falls, upper and lower; they are the largest in Indiana.

This is one of Indiana's amazing natural sites. The falls are a result of pre-glacial bedrock located underneath lake sediments from the Illinoisan glacial period. The Lieber and Cataract Falls SRA is managed by the Indiana Department of Natural Resources. In addition to Cataract Falls, the SRA offers trails, camping, an aquatics center, boat access, horseshoe pits, basketball courts, and play areas. Pack a picnic for lunch with a relaxing view of the falls in the background.

2605 N Cataract Rd., Spencer, (765) 276-0194
on.in.gov/liebersra

TIP

Visit the Cataract General Store, located just down the road from Cataract Falls. It was built in 1860 and is the oldest general store in Indiana.
2799 S Cataract Rd., Spencer, (765) 795-4782
cataract-general-store.business.site

INDIANA STATE PARK AND FOREST WATERFALLS

Indiana is home to more than 15 waterfalls. They are located throughout the state, and many of them can be found along Indiana state park and forest hiking trails.

Charlestown State Park
12500 State Rd. 62, Charlestown, (812) 256-5600
on.in.gov/charlestownsp

Clifty Falls State Park
2221 Clifty Dr., Madison, (812) 273-8885
on.in.gov/cliftyfallssp

McCormick's Creek State Park
250 McCormick's Creek Park Rd., Spencer, (812) 829-2235
on.in.gov/mccormickscreeksp

Salamonie River State Forest
5400 E Salamonie Forest Rd., Lagro, (260) 782-0430
on.in.gov/salamonieriversf

Shades State Park
7751 S 890 W, Waveland, (765) 435-2810
on.in.gov/shadessp

Spring Mill State Park
3333 State Rd. 60 E, Mitchell, (812) 849-3534
on.in.gov/springmillsp

Turkey Run State Park
8121 E Park Rd., Marshall, (765) 597-2635
on.in.gov/turkeyrunsp

HOWL WITH THE WOLVES
AT WOLF PARK

I've had one chance in my lifetime to howl with wolves, and that opportunity happened at Wolf Park in Battle Ground. Located just outside of Lafayette, this wolf sanctuary is a nonprofit education, conservation, and research facility that rescues wolves and other wild animals. Visitors are invited to tour the facility during specific times.

The Howl Night tour takes place in the evening when the wolves are more active. Guests are encouraged to howl along with the wolves during a demonstration given by animal curators. The wolves love snacks and playing with cardboard boxes. It's an interactive tour for all ages. Before the demonstration, you have the opportunity to walk around the park and see some of the other animal enclosures.

4004 E 800 N, Battle Ground, (765) 567-2265
wolfpark.org

VISIT INDIANA WOLF RESCUES

Red Wolf Sanctuary
3027 State Rd. 262, Rising Sun, (812) 438-2306
redwolf.org

Wolf Creek Habitat & Rescue
14099 Wolf Creek Rd., Brookville, (765) 647-4735
wolfcreekhabitat.org

40

RACE DOWN THE TOBOGGAN RUN
AT POKAGON STATE PARK

Are you ready for a thrill ride? A 90-foot vertical drop and 20- to 30-second rides offer an adrenaline rush and have adults and kids alike eagerly wanting to ride again. The refrigerated toboggan run at Pokagon State Park in northeast Indiana is open seasonally, with or without snow, from November to February. The toboggan slide has been entertaining visitors since 1935, with upgrades and repairs made over the decades.

Up to four people can ride on one toboggan. With two slides, two toboggans can slide at the same time. There is a warming station on location with concessions and restrooms. Toboggans are available on a first-come, first-served basis for a rental fee. Dress warmly and bring thick gloves; it's a cool and fast ride down the slide!

450 Lane 100 Lake James, Angola, (260) 833-2012
on.in.gov/pokagonsp

TIP

Cross-country ski rentals are also available at Pokagon State Park.

41

TAKE YOURSELF OUT TO A BALL GAME
AT PARKVIEW FIELD

Fort Wayne knows baseball; the first-ever professional baseball game was played there in 1871 at Memorial Stadium. When Memorial Stadium closed in 2008, Parkview Field came alive. Parkview is home to the Fort Wayne TinCaps baseball team and is the number one minor league ballpark in the country.

Tickets to a TinCaps game are relatively affordable. Post-game fireworks wrap up every home game and are fun for the kids. It's a great outing for families and one of the cleanest ballparks I've been to. In addition to baseball, Parkview Field hosts events like concerts, fundraisers, and festivals. You can rent it for a birthday party! When not in use, the field is open as a public park from 7 a.m. to sunset.

1301 Ewing St., Fort Wayne, (260) 482-6400
parkviewfield.com

THE BEST HOOSIER BALLPARKS

Bosse Field
Filming site for *A League of Their Own*; home of the Evansville Otters.
23 Don Mattingly Way, Evansville, (812) 435-8686

Four Winds Field
Home of the South Bend Cubs.
501 W South St., South Bend, (574) 235-9988

League Stadium
Filming site for *A League of Their Own*; home of the Dubois County Bombers.
203 S Cherry St., Huntingburg, (812) 683-3700

US Steel Yard
Home of the Gary SouthShore RailCats.
1 Stadium Plaza, Gary, (219) 882-2255

Victory Field
Home of the Indianapolis Indians.
501 W Maryland St., Indianapolis, (317) 269-3545

SCOUT OUT SOME BISON
AT KANKAKEE SANDS

Most people don't associate prairies or bison with Indiana, and that is what makes Kankakee Sands so unique. It's one of the only places in Indiana where you can hike through prairies and see wild bison roaming (safely separated from you by fencing). The Efroymson Restoration at Kankakee Sands is over 8,000 acres of wetlands and prairies managed by the Nature Conservancy of Indiana. This land is home to more than 86 rare and endangered species, 240 bird species, and 600 native plants. The bison can best be seen from the Bison Viewing Area (open 7 a.m. to dusk), and I've spotted them while driving around Kankakee Sands as well.

Five self-guided hiking trails loop through the prairie, wetlands, Kankakee Sands, and oak savanna. Don't forget to bring a pair of binoculars.

3294 N US-41, Morocco, (219) 285-2184
nature.org/en-us/get-involved/how-to-help/places-we-protect/kankakee-sands

TIP

Kankakee Sands is rural. Port-a-potties are available in the Bison Viewing Area. Bring along snacks and drinks for your visit.

INDIANA BISON VIEWING LOCATIONS

Broken Wagon Bison
Bison tours, meat, and goods.
563 W 450 N, Hobart, (219) 759-3523
brokenwagonbison.com

Cook's Bison Ranch
83-acre bison farm with tours, wagon rides, and Buffalo Treasures Gift Shop.
5645 E 600 S, Wolcottville, (866) 382-2356
cooksbisonranch.com

Ouabache State Park
Contains a 20-acre American bison exhibit.
4930 E State Rd. 201, Bluffton, (260) 824-0926
on.in.gov/ouabachesp

Wild Winds Buffalo Preserve
Home to over 250 wild bison; offers tours, lodging, and a gift shop.
6975 N Ray Rd., Fremont, (260) 495-0137
wildwindsbuffalo.com

43

FLOAT DOWN
THE TIPPECANOE RIVER

Summer in Indiana doesn't feel complete without a float trip down the gentle Tippecanoe River. This river offers a slow and relaxing ride for kayaks, canoes, rafts, and tubes. The Tippecanoe is like a giant, natural lazy river. It's perfect for a float trip. Riverside Rentals is the best option for rentals along the Tippecanoe River. It provides transportation to your drop-off location, and you float directly back to Riverside Rentals, where your vehicle is parked. Float trips can last between three and six hours, depending on the type of trip you choose. Overnight upstream kayak trips with a stay at Tippecanoe River State Park are a fun option for those looking for more time on the water.

Riverside Rentals
589 E Old State Rd. 14, Winamac, (574) 946-3142
riversidecanoes.com

TIP

Bring water shoes; they are required for the float trips. I recommend renting the cooler float and bringing your own cooler with food and drinks.

INDIANA KAYAK, CANOE, AND TUBE FLOAT TRIPS

Clements Canoes Outdoor Center
8295 W State Rd. 234, Waveland, (765) 435-2070
clementscanoes.com

Sugar Creek Campground
841 W 83 N, Crawfordsville, (765) 362-5528
sugarcreekcanoetrips.com

Sugar Valley Canoe Trips
1313 IN-47, Marshall, (765) 597-2364
sugarvalleycanoes.com

White River Canoe Company
17180 River Rd., Noblesville, (317) 867-4233
whiterivercanoe.com

44

EXPLORE THE UNDERGROUND WORLD
OF MARENGO CAVE

In 1883 a 15-year-old girl and her brother discovered Marengo Cave. Within just a few days, the landowner was offering public tours, and the cave has been open to visitors ever since. This natural wonder is phenomenal to see in person; you'll discover different types of cave formations and dwellers. The cave chambers have been used to hold church services, meetings, weddings, and concerts, and movies have been filmed here. The cave remains a cool 52 degrees year-round. In 1984, it was named a US National Natural Landmark.

There are two walking tours: the Crystal Palace and the Dripstone Trail. I suggest purchasing combo tickets for both tours; it is just under two hours in length. Cave exploring is available for those looking to get muddy while crawling through undeveloped, natural caves. This is not recommended for younger children or anyone with claustrophobia.

400 E State Rd. 64, Marengo, (812) 365-2705
marengocave.com

TIP

You can stay overnight at the Marengo Cave Campground, located on site.

THE INDIANA CAVE TRAIL

Pick up an Indiana Cave Trail passport at Marengo Cave or any of these locations. Have your passport stamped at each site to earn a free T-shirt.
indianacavetrail.com

Bluespring Caverns
One-hour cave boat tour.
1459 Blue Spring Caverns Rd., Bedford, (812) 279-9471
bluespringcaverns.com

Indiana Caverns
Indiana's longest cave.
1267 Green Acres Dr. SW, Corydon, (812) 734-1200
indianacaverns.com

Squire Boone Caverns
Caverns with the largest rimstone dams are accessible to the public.
100 Squire Boone Rd. SW, Mauckport, (812) 732-4381
squireboonecaverns.com

JOURNEY AROUND THE WORLD

AT THE FORT WAYNE CHILDREN'S ZOO

If you love animals, you'll love the Fort Wayne Children's Zoo. It's small but mighty and has opportunities for up-close encounters with the Animal Experiences. It has not only been voted one of Indiana's best zoos but also has been ranked as one of the top zoos in the nation. It is situated in Fort Wayne's Franke Park, with 40 acres and over 1,000 animals. You can take a journey around the world to different habitats, such as Africa, Australia, and the Indonesian rain forest. Of course, the Indiana Family Farm is a local favorite.

Plan to spend at least three to four hours here. The Sky Safari is worth the extra fee for a slow, quiet ride overlooking the zoo. My favorite things to do here are feeding the giraffes, watching the sea lions, and visiting the orangutans.

3411 Sherman Blvd., Fort Wayne, (260) 427-6800
kidszoo.org

TIP

The zoo is a certified sensory-inclusive facility. It has sensory bags, headphones, and quiet spaces available for those who need them.

EXTRAORDINARY INDIANA ZOOS

Indianapolis Zoo
1200 W Washington St., Indianapolis, (317) 630-2001
indianapoliszoo.com

Mesker Park Zoo & Botanic Garden
1545 Mesker Park Dr., Evansville, (812) 435-6143
meskerparkzoo.com

Potawatomi Zoo
500 S Greenlawn Ave., South Bend, (574) 235-9800
potawatomizoo.org

Washington Park Zoo
115 Lake Shore Dr., Michigan City, (219) 873-1510
washingtonparkzoo.com

TROT THE TRAILS
AT TURKEY RUN STATE PARK

All the Indiana state parks are amazing, but I've selected the trails at Turkey Run State Park for its famous geological formations and canyons. It is a forested area that follows Sugar Creek. Eleven marked trails range from easy to very rugged. The trails wander through deep canyons, cliff edges, streambeds, an old quarry, a coal mine, and some of the most scenic views in the state. The most rugged trails require ladder climbing and may be impassable during high waters.

Cross the suspension bridge over Sugar Creek to access most of the trails in the canyon areas. This is where the popular Punch Bowl, climbing ladders, and rock formations can be found. The sights are unbelievable; it doesn't feel as if you are in Indiana anymore.

8121 E Park Rd., Marshall, (765) 597-2635
on.in.gov/turkeyrunsp

TIP

Also visit Shades State Park, located just over 10 miles from Turkey Run State Park. 7751 S 890 W, Waveland, (765) 435-2810, on.in.gov/shadessp

POUR AND TOUR
AT THE SCULPTURE TRAILS OUTDOOR MUSEUM

More than 100 large sculptures are located along a three-mile wooded trail at the Sculpture Trails Outdoor Museum. These sculptures were created by artists from all around the world. The trails are moderately rugged, and they are free to visit if you opt for a self-guided tour. If you can't access the trails, you can call ahead to schedule a golf-cart tour. The museum's art education program offers workshops and programs for anyone interested in pouring, blacksmithing, or metal arts. An old barn provides a place for workshops and programs.

You're guaranteed to snag Instagram-worthy photos with these particular and imaginative life-sized sculptures. Bring a camera and a friend!

6764 N Tree Farm Rd., Solsberry, (502) 554-1788
sculpturetrails.com

TIP

Visit the Yoho General Store for breakfast, lunch, dinner, and goods. The store has been serving the Solsberry community since the 1930s. 10043 E Tulip Rd., Solsberry, (812) 825-7834, yohogeneralstore.com

48

DIVE, SWIM, FISH, AND CAMP
AT WHITE ROCK PARK

This popular St. Paul swimming hole is the best cliff diving location in Indiana. It's the perfect place to show off your jumping skills and compete in making the biggest splash. White Rock Park is a veteran-owned campground located on a natural quarry southeast of Indianapolis. The quarry creates a nice ledge for cliff diving, which is one of the main attractions at the park. Ladders along the side of the quarry make it easy to climb up the sides. Swimming, fishing, and scuba diving are other available activities.

Primitive campsites are available for up to eight people (and three tents) and include a fireplace ring and picnic table. Kids camp for free with parents, and catch and release fishing is included with camping.

7080 S 750 E, Saint Paul, (765) 525-3483
whiterockpark.com

TIP

Bring cash. There is a service charge to use a credit card.

BEST SWIMMING SPOTS

Brookville Lake
14108 State Rd. 101, Brookville, (765) 647-2657
on.in.gov/brookvillelake

Fairfax State Recreation Area
4850 S State Rd. 446, Bloomington, (812) 837-9546
on.in.gov/monroelake

Potawatomi Inn Beach
Pokagon State Park
450 Lane 100 Lake James, Angola, (260) 833-2012
on.in.gov/pokagonsp

Salamonie Lake
9214 Lost Bridge Rd. W, Andrews, (260) 468-2125
on.in.gov/salamonielake

Summit Lake State Park
5993 N Messick Rd., New Castle, (765) 766-5873
on.in.gov/summitlakesp

RENT AND RIDE A 19TH-CENTURY CAROUSEL
AT RIVERSIDE PARK

The Cass County Dentzel Carousel was handcrafted by Gustav Dentzel, whom imported the United States' first known merry-go-round. Dentzel hand-carved all the animals on the carousel. Today it is a National Historic Landmark and sits inside the McHale Community Complex in Logansport. It is open Memorial Day to Labor Day, and visitors can ride the carousel for only a dollar! A historic, restored miniature train is located outside the building and also offers rides.

During non-operating hours, the carousel can be rented by the hour. For an affordable rate, you can have unlimited use of a historic, 19th-century carousel. How unique is that? If that isn't a bucket list-worthy item, I don't know what is.

1208 Riverside Dr., Logansport, (574) 753-8725
casscountycarousel.com

LIFE IS LIKE A CAROUSEL; ENJOY THE RIDE

Take a ride on a historic carousel. There are several on display around the state.

1906 Dentzel Carousel at Davis Mercantile
225 N Harrison St., Shipshewana, (260) 768-7300
davismercantile.com

"Carousel Wishes and Dreams" at The Children's Museum of Indianapolis
3000 N Meridian St., Indianapolis, (317) 334-4000
childrensmuseum.org/exhibits/carousel

Engelbrecht Carousel at the Mesker Park Zoo
1545 Mesker Park Dr., Evansville, (812) 435-6143
meskerparkzoo.com

"Little Beauty" Carousel at Forest Park
701 Cicero Rd., Noblesville, (317) 776-6350
noblesvilleparks.org/212/carousel-corner

INTERACT WITH THE PIGS

AT OINKING ACRES FARM RESCUE & SANCTUARY

Olivia Head was only 14 years old when she adopted her first pig. Eventually she would turn her family farm into a sanctuary for unwanted potbellied pigs and become the founder of Oinking Acres Farm Rescue & Sanctuary. Since 2017, over 300 neglected, abused, and unwanted pigs have been rescued. Take a tour to meet, feed, and interact with the pigs. Tour tickets can be purchased online.

It's hard not to fall in love with the residents at Oinking Acres. While some of the pigs are permanent members of the farm, they need sponsors, and most of the pigs are available for adoption. The growing farm also includes a few rescued cows, goats, bunnies, and birds. You won't be able to go on a tour without wanting to adopt a new potbellied friend!

8420 N County Rd. 650 E, Brownsburg, (317) 225-1761
oinkingacres.org

FARM ANIMAL RESCUES YOU CAN VISIT AND TOUR

Erin's Farm
5200 S Liverpool Rd., Hobart
(773) 575-4990
erinsfarm.net

Uplands Peak Sanctuary
6444 Freedom Arney Rd., Freedom
(812) 896-2114
uplandspeaksanctuary.org

TIP

Wear closed-toed shoes or boots and bring some fruits or veggies if you'd like to feed the pigs. They love cucumbers, carrots, and apples.

BOTTLEWORKS HOTEL (page 157)

MONASTERY IMMACULATE CONCEPTION (page 133)

BISON AT OUABACHE STATE PARK (page 67)

CENTURY OF PROGRESS HOMES (page 114)

CATARACT FALLS (page 60)

TURKEY RUN STATE PARK (page 74)

FORT WAYNE CHILDREN'S ZOO (page 72)

TARDIS AT WHO NORTH AMERICA (page 148)

CHILDREN'S MUSEUM OF INDIANAPOLIS (page 98)

WEST BADEN SPRINGS HOTEL (page 108)

MILLER HOUSE AND GARDEN (page 114)

ABANDONED ROSE ISLAND AMUSEMENT PARK (page 121)

STUDEBAKER NATIONAL MUSEUM (page 122)

DAVIS MERCANTILE (page 142)

PLAY LIKE A CHAMP
AT THE UNIVERSITY OF NOTRE DAME

South Bend is proud to be home to the Notre Dame Fighting Irish, the athletic teams that represent the University of Notre Dame. Going to a football game at the Notre Dame stadium is a different experience than any other college, or even NFL, game I've ever been to. The pre-kickoff campus excitement, traditions, and crowd are energizing. Whether they win or lose, it's always a great time.

In addition to football, Notre Dame's basketball and hockey are popular games to attend. Historic stadium tours are also offered publicly and privately. On the tour, you get to see the stadium, hear about past and present iconic venues in sports, and walk on the field. You also get to touch the "Play Like a Champion" sign (a Notre Dame tradition).

2010 Moose Krause Cir., Notre Dame, (574) 631-5036
und.com

TIP

The university campus is gorgeous. Take a free, self-guided tour to see the Snite Museum of Art, Grotto of Our Lady of Lourdes, Basilica of the Sacred Heart, Golden Dome administration building, and *Touchdown Jesus* mural.

HANG OUT WITH THE DINOS

AT THE CHILDREN'S MUSEUM OF INDIANAPOLIS

Plan to spend an entire day at The Children's Museum of Indianapolis. It has five floors of interactive exhibits, plus the outdoor Sports Legends Experience and the newly revamped Dinosphere exhibit. There are things to do for all ages, from toddlers to adults, at this popular museum. My teenagers even enjoy the Sports Legends Experience. And adults find themselves roaming the museum without kids during the popular After Dark events.

Dinosphere features five immersive experiences and lets guests get up close to dinosaurs and talk to real scientists. Other popular exhibits include the story of Anne Frank, National Geographic Treasures of the Earth, the largest water clock in the United States, the Playscape area for younger children, and the Schaefer Planetarium. Let the little ones march in the End of the Day Parade with Rex, the mascot.

3000 N Meridian St., Indianapolis, (317) 334-4000
childrensmuseum.org

TIP

Parking is free in the parking garages adjacent to the museum.

CONQUER INDIANA'S LONGEST HIKING TRAIL

ON THE KNOBSTONE TRAIL

Surprisingly, Knobstone Trail is not the most discussed trail in Indiana, despite being the longest trail and having some of the best scenic views. This makes it one of the state's best-kept secrets. Referred to as the "Appalachian Trail of Indiana," it is 60 miles in length and spreads out over three counties in southern Indiana. The rather rugged terrain crosses paths with Clark State Forest, Elk Creek Public Fishing Area, and Jackson-Washington State Forest. With the difficulty of maintaining such a large trail, several steep climbs, and erosion, it is a difficult trail to hike. However, Knobstone can easily be hiked in sections if you aren't an experienced hiker or backpacker.

The most scenic views can be found at the Knobstone Escarpment, located between Normal and Seymour.

Clark, Scott, and Washington Counties, (812) 358-2160
in.gov/dnr/forestry/properties/knobstone-trail-conditions-reroutes-maps

RIDE THE COASTERS AND WAVES AT HOLIDAY WORLD AND SPLASHIN' SAFARI

Most people don't expect to find Santa in southern Indiana, but there is an entire town named after him. In Santa Claus, a holiday-themed amusement park has been entertaining families since 1946. Holiday World and Splashin' Safari are two parks in one. The theme park, Holiday World, has roller coasters and other rides, including the nation's first launched-wing coaster and one of the largest and fastest wooden roller coasters in the world. In 1993, the Splashin' Safari water park was added, with wave pools, a lazy river, and 10+ water slides. Four generations of the same family have operated the parks since the beginning.

It's an extremely clean and family-friendly destination. Several freebies come with admission, including unlimited fountain drinks, water, Gatorade, lemonade, sunscreen, hand sanitizer, Wi-Fi, and parking.

452 E Christmas Blvd., Santa Claus, (877) 463-2645
holidayworld.com

Indiana Beach Amusement and Water Park is located in northwest Indiana on Lake Shafer in Monticello. It's also a two-in-one amusement and water park and is a long-standing Indiana gem.

5224 E Indiana Beach Rd., Monticello
(574) 583-4141
indianabeach.com

RETREAT TO A RAIN FOREST

AT GARFIELD PARK CONSERVATORY AND GARDENS

Garfield Park is Indianapolis's oldest park. The 136-acre green space consists of beautiful sunken gardens and a 10,000-square-foot rainforest-themed conservatory. The conservatory was built in 1915 and rebuilt in 1959. During the cold Indiana months, a visit to the conservatory is a welcome escape to a warm, humid, and tropical paradise. Brick paths lead you through the rain forest of ferns, palms, orchids, bananas, coffee, and more. Sit on the benches and enjoy the waterfall and koi pond.

Events, tours, and workshops are offered at the conservatory and in the gardens for both adults and children. The outdoor sunken gardens are free to visit all year. Have your camera ready because the three acres of fountains, flower beds, and architecture make a great backdrop, especially in the spring and summer.

2505 Conservatory Dr., Indianapolis, (317) 327-7183
garfieldgardensconservatory.org

ESCAPE TO BEAUTIFUL BOTANICAL GARDENS

Azalea Path Arboretum and Botanical Gardens
1502 N County Rd. 825 W, Hazleton, (812) 640-9133
azaleapatharboretum.org

Foellinger-Freimann Botanical Conservatory
1100 S Calhoun St., Fort Wayne, (260) 427-6440
botanicalconservatory.org

Friendship Botanic Gardens
2055 E US Hwy. 12, Michigan City, (219) 878-9885
friendshipbotanicgardens.org

Wellfield Botanic Gardens
1011 N Main St., Elkhart, (574) 266-2006, ext. 105
wellfieldgardens.org

Old Cathedral Catholic Church

CULTURE AND HISTORY

OBSERVE THE CITY SKYLINE

FROM THE TOP OF THE SOLDIERS AND SAILORS MONUMENT

Monument Circle in downtown Indianapolis is a roundabout that wraps around the Soldiers and Sailors Monument. This is the official state memorial honoring Indiana veterans who served in the Revolutionary War, the War of 1812, the Mexican War, the Civil War, the Frontier Wars, and the Spanish-American War. It reaches 284 feet and has an observatory at the top with panoramic views of Indianapolis. It's a must to get a picture in front of the monument.

You can go inside the monument; a small gift shop is located on the main level. It's free to visit the observatory if you climb the 330 steep and winding stairs. You can also pay a small fee to ride the elevator to nearly the top (always free for veterans and military members). It's worth the small fee if you have a fear of heights or a difficult time with stairs.

1 Monument Cir., Indianapolis
in.gov/iwm/soldiers-and-sailors-monument

The Soldiers and Sailors Monument is located in the Indiana World War Memorial Plaza Historic District. Among US cities, Indianapolis is second only to Washington, DC, in the number of monuments dedicated to veterans and military conflicts.

57

ESCAPE TO LUXURY
AT THE HISTORIC FRENCH LICK RESORT

French Lick Resort is iconic to Indiana's history. In the early 1900s, the resort was where all the wealthy and affluent folks sojourned. Famous individuals like Al Capone, Richard Nixon, and Louis Armstrong are known to have stayed there. The resort consists of a casino and three hotels. Prior to becoming a resort area, the mineral springs and salt licks attracted animals and made a popular spot for hunting.

The West Baden Springs Hotel later became known as the "Eighth Wonder of the World" for an atrium that spans 200 feet in diameter; it was the world's largest free-span dome until the 1960s. It's a wonder to see in person! Book an atrium-view room; the view is worth every penny.

Visitors can stay overnight, eat like royalty, and participate in many resort activities. Free 24/7 shuttle and trolley transportation takes guests around the resort and the local community.

8670 W State Rd. 56, French Lick, (888) 936-9360
frenchlick.com

TIP

French Lick Resort is even more magical during the holiday season. It lights up with over half a million lights, festive displays, and activities. You'll want to book your reservations in advance.

58

HONOR EVA'S STORY

AT CANDLES HOLOCAUST MUSEUM AND EDUCATION CENTER

Do you know the story of Eva Mozes Kor? After surviving the Holocaust, Kor married and moved to Terre Haute. There she founded the CANDLES Holocaust Museum and Education Center—a place to educate others about the Holocaust and prevent prejudice. It is the only Holocaust museum in Indiana. In 2003 the museum was burned down by an arsonist, but through the support of the community it was rebuilt in 2005. The hate crime only strengthened Kor's message, that "light prevails over darkness, and love will always conquer hate."

Plan for two hours to visit the museum. The tour is self-guided, but docents are available to answer questions. Exhibits are appropriate for children aged middle school and older. Admission is free for veterans.

1532 S 3rd St., Terre Haute, (812) 234-7881
candlesholocaustmuseum.org

COMMEMORATE HOOSIER HERITAGE AT THE INDIANA STATE MUSEUM

A list of the top things to do in Indiana isn't complete without the actual state museum. The Indiana State Museum is one of my favorite museums. It is located in downtown Indianapolis, but the museum also oversees 12 historic sites throughout Indiana, many of which are included in this book.

The museum's permanent galleries and rotating exhibits span from prehistoric times to the present. There are three floors of exhibits and galleries with art, history, science, and architecture. Make sure to see Fred; he's the popular 13,000-year-old mastodon in the Frozen Reign gallery. The state museum also hosts regular events and programs for adults, children, homeschoolers, and families.

650 W Washington St., Indianapolis, (317) 232-1637
indianamuseum.org

TIP

Check out the Eugene and Marilyn Glick Indiana History Center to explore more of Indiana's rich history. It is located along the Canal Walk, a few blocks from the Indiana State Museum. 450 W Ohio St., Indianapolis, (317) 232-1882, indianahistory.org

GROW UP WITH ABE
AT THE LINCOLN BOYHOOD NATIONAL MEMORIAL

Abraham Lincoln lived in southern Indiana from the ages of 7 to 21. The Lincoln Boyhood National Memorial preserves the president's boyhood home. A free visit to the national park invites you to see the Memorial Visitor Center, the Lincoln Living Historical Farm, the cabin site memorial, and Nancy Lincoln's grave and to hike the Boyhood Trail or the Trail of Twelve Stones.

On the Lincoln Living Historical Farm, rangers dress in period clothing and portray what a typical farm day would have been like in the 1820s. The rangers demonstrate farming activities and talk with visitors. The farm is open seven days a week, April to September. The memorial, trails, and sights are open all year, with the exception of holidays.

3027 E South St., Lincoln City, (812) 937-4541
nps.gov/libo/index.htm

TIP

Lincoln State Park is located directly across the street from the Lincoln Boyhood National Memorial. The state park has a beach, trails, cabins, and camping. 15476 County Rd. 300 E, Lincoln City, (812) 937-4710
on.in.gov/lincolnsp

61

REPORT FOR DUTY
AT THE INDIANA MILITARY MUSEUM

The most inclusive and extensive collection of military artifacts in the world is found at the Indiana Military Museum. I've never seen a more organized museum, with collections arranged in chronological order, starting with the Civil War. Exhibits include weapons, uniforms, vehicles, armor, and aircraft. Look for unique artifacts such as Edith Shain's nurse's cap (the nurse who was photographed in Times Square kissing the sailor on V-J Day) and a hand-knitted afghan made by General Custer's wife.

In addition to the museum, a 22,000-square-foot annex features WWI through post-Vietnam War exhibits. Battle reenactments and demonstrations throughout the year bring visitors and excitement to the Vincennes community.

715 S 6th St., Vincennes, (812) 882-1941
indymilitary.com

TIP

Visit the nearby Red Skelton Museum of American Comedy. The comedian was from Vincennes, and his WWII uniform and other memorabilia are also featured at the Indiana Military Museum.
20 Red Skelton Blvd., Vincennes, (812) 888-4184 redskeltonmuseum.org

GET A HISTORY LESSON
AT THE CORYDON CAPITOL STATE HISTORIC SITE

Corydon became Indiana's first state capital when Indiana leveled up from a territory to a state in 1816. In 1825 the capital moved to Indianapolis. The first Capitol building was located in downtown Corydon and built with limestone from local Indiana quarries.

You can take a guided tour of the Capitol building through the Indiana State Museum. The tour also includes a visit to the Governor's Headquarters and the Porter Law Office. You can take a self-guided tour instead, but you won't be able to go inside the buildings.

The famous Constitution Elm is within walking distance of the Capitol building. It is believed to be the tree where the 43 Indiana Constitutional Convention delegates met to draft Indiana's first constitution.

202 E Walnut St., Corydon, (812) 738-4890
indianamuseum.org/historic-sites/corydon-capitol

63

GO BACK TO THE FUTURE
WITH A TOUR OF THE CENTURY OF PROGRESS HOMES

In 1933 the Chicago World's Fair assembled dozens of futuristic homes for an exhibit called the Century of Progress. These homes look futuristic even today; one has glass walls and an airplane hangar. After the fair, five of those homes were sold and transferred by barge and trucks to Beverly Shores, Indiana. They were the beginning of a new lakeside resort community, but when the resort failed the National Park Service took over the homes in the 1960s. Through a partnership, the homes are leased to individuals who agree to rehabilitate the properties.

Homes can be viewed from the roadside at any time. But once a year, in September, you have an opportunity to tour the homes. These are guided tours. But you've got to be quick; tickets sell out fast!

Indiana Dunes Visitor Center
1100 N Mineral Springs Rd., Porter, (219) 395-1882
nps.gov/indu/learn/historyculture/centuryofprogress.htm

TOUR MID-CENTURY INDIANA HOMES
Frank Lloyd Wright's Samara
1301 Woodland Ave., West Lafayette, (765) 409-5522
samara-house.org

Miller House and Garden
506 5th St., Columbus, (812) 378-2622
columbus.in.us/miller-house-and-garden-tour

DISCOVER THE SECRET HIDING SPOTS IN THE LEVI & CATHARINE COFFIN HOUSE

Levi and Catharine Coffin weren't just any ordinary Hoosiers; they were Quaker abolitionists who helped thousands of enslaved persons seeking refuge. Their brick home in Fountain City was built in 1939 and became known as the "Grand Central Station of the Underground Railroad." For 20 years they helped freedom seekers escape to Canada from the South. The original Coffin home is still standing as a State Historic Site—it's incredible to see in person.

The tour starts with a visit to the interpretive center and includes artifacts and hiding spaces in the home. Watch the presentation video before touring the home. It's an amazing story of two selfless humanitarians.

201 US Hwy. 27 N, Fountain City, (765) 847-1691
indianamuseum.org/historic-sites/levi-catharine-coffin-house

CRUISE THE CANAL
ON THE *DELPHI*

In 1850, waterways were the highways of today. The *Delphi* is a replicated canal boat that takes passengers on narrated tours down the Wabash and Erie Canal as it was in the 1850s. The anecdotal cruises are 40 minutes long and offered from May to September in Canal Park. Cruises are available first come, first serve on the weekends; you may call for a reservation during the week. Private cruises are welcome for groups who book in advance.

The park includes other historic attractions, such as the Reed Case House, an interpretive center, and an 1850s Pioneer Village. You can purchase a discounted combination ticket at the interpretive center.

1030 N Washington St., Delphi, (765) 564-2870
wabashanderiecanal.org/canal-boat-cruises-delphi-indiana

TIP

Visit Delphi in early July during its annual Canal Days festival. Canal boat rides are available, and interactive activities take place throughout the park.

REFLECT
AT THE SHRINE OF CHRIST'S PASSION

In 2001 an enormous, half-mile outdoor prayer trail was built to offer the public a place to take a journey through the last days of Jesus Christ's life. The Shrine of Christ's Passion is tucked in a suburban corner of Northwest Indiana, surrounded by gardens. It took 10 years and $10 million to build. There is no admission fee, and people from all walks of life and faiths are welcome. The trail is interactive and contains 40 life-sized bronze sculptures with audio recordings telling stories from the Bible.

The Moses at Mount Sinai portion of the trail took three years to build and features sounds and lighting effects. The gift shop is 12,000 square feet and contains thousands of items. There's also a café with beverages and snacks, an art gallery, and a library.

10630 Wicker Ave., St. John, (219) 365-6010
shrineofchristspassion.org

TIP

The prayer trail is ADA accessible, and wheelchairs are available; please call ahead to reserve.

MARVEL IN AN AUTHOR'S WONDERLAND AT LIMBERLOST

Have you heard of the novel *A Girl of the Limberlost* by Indiana author Gene Stratton-Porter? It was one of her best-selling novels and was inspired by the Limberlost Swamp, located near the Limberlost State Historic Site. J. K. Rowling has said that *A Girl of the Limberlost* was one of her favorite books as a child and tweeted in 2020 that she wanted to visit Limberlost. The Limberlost Cabin, where Stratton-Porter lived and wrote six of her novels, is located on the site. Stratton-Porter loved the outdoors and nature; she spent time in the swamp gathering ideas for her novels and taking photos. The swamp was drained for farmland in 1913, however, and the family relocated to the shore of Sylvan Lake near Rome City.

Begin your journey at the visitor center for a tour of the cabin and grounds. Bring comfortable shoes to hike the Loblolly Marsh before or afterward.

Limberlost State Historic Site
200 6th St., Geneva, (260) 368-7428
indianamuseum.org/historic-sites/limberlost

DID YOU KNOW?

In 1913, Stratton-Porter moved to the Cabin at Wildflower Woods, now an Indiana State Historic Site in Rome City. You can also visit this cabin, which has a garden, forests, and trails.

Gene Stratton-Porter State Historic Site
1205 Pleasant Point, Rome City, (260) 854-3790
indianamuseum.org/historic-sites/gene-stratton-porter

JOIN A RANGER FOR A TOUR

OF THE CLARK MEMORIAL

Vincennes is a small town packed full of history. It is home to one of three national parks in Indiana, the George Rogers Clark National Historical Park. The park honors George Rogers Clark and his troops for their victory over the British at Fort Sackville. The park and memorial are located where Fort Sackville once stood. To see the inside of the memorial building, it is worth taking the ranger tour. The building is 80 feet tall, and the walls are two feet thick. The memorial is made of granite, and a rotunda inside is surrounded by several murals.

Start at the visitor center. A 30-minute film shown in the theater is helpful to watch before touring the memorial.

George Rogers Clark National Historical Park
401 S 2nd St., Vincennes, (812) 882-1776
nps.gov/gero/index.htm

WANDER THROUGH
THE ABANDONED ROSE ISLAND AMUSEMENT PARK

An abandoned 1920s amusement park is located on a peninsula in Charlestown State Park. A bridge connects the park to the peninsula and gives explorers a chance to take a trail through the former amusement park. Although Rose Island consists mostly of ruins, there are still unique remnants of history and interpretive signs at each of the sites. There are rumors that the area is haunted by ghosts of the amusement park's past. Spooky!

The island and trails are free to visit, with admission to the state park. Rose Island is located on Trail 7 and accessible by taking Trail 3. Keep in mind that Trail 3 is rugged and has a very steep road that requires some endurance. It's a good workout even for those who are in shape.

Charlestown State Park
12500 State Rd. 62, Charlestown, (812) 256-5600
on.in.gov/charlestownsp

SPOT A NATIONAL TREASURE

AT THE STUDEBAKER NATIONAL MUSEUM

The Studebakers are famous worldwide and have forged a lasting legacy in automotive and industrial history. The company was once the world's largest producer of horse-drawn vehicles; it later manufactured automobiles. In 1966 production was halted, and 33 vehicles were donated to the City of South Bend. These vehicles were used to create the Studebaker National Museum. Included in the donation was the world's largest collection of US presidential carriages, including the carriage that Abraham Lincoln used on the night of his assassination. It is displayed in the National Treasures exhibit.

Plan to spend two to three hours at the museum. There are three permanent exhibits, a rotating exhibit, and an interactive exhibit for the kids. Don't forget to get your photo with the Studebaker on display!

201 Chapin St., South Bend, (574) 235-9714
studebakermuseum.org

TIP

The History Museum is connected to the Studebaker National Museum. You can purchase a discounted combo ticket to visit both museums.

INDIANA AUTOMOBILE MUSEUMS

Auburn Cord Duesenberg Automobile Museum
1600 S Wayne St., Auburn, (260) 925-1444
automobilemuseum.org

Early Ford V-8 Foundation Museum
2181 Rotunda Dr., Auburn, (260) 927-8022
fordv8foundation.org

Indianapolis Motor Speedway Museum
4750 W 16th St., Indianapolis, (317) 492-6784
imsmuseum.org

Model T Museum
309 N 8th St., Richmond, (765) 373-3106
mtfca.com/museum

National Auto & Truck Museum
1000 Gordon M. Buehrig Pl., Auburn, (260) 925-9100
natmus.org

STEP FOOT ON SACRED GROUND
AT CROWN HILL CEMETERY

The best view of Indianapolis is from the hill in Crown Hill Cemetery. This also happens to be the final resting place of some of the most influential and affluent historical figures in Indiana. Hoosier poet James Whitcomb Riley is buried at the very top of the hill. President Benjamin Harrison and the legendary John Dillinger are buried at Crown Hill, as well.

This is the third-largest non-governmental cemetery in the United States. Throughout this cultural landmark, you'll find notable names, wildlife, trees, and an 1875 Gothic Chapel.

The cemetery is open to the public daily. Self-guided tour maps are available online, and guided tours are available throughout the year.

700 W 38th St., Indianapolis, (317) 920-4165
crownhillhf.org

TIP

There are two entrances to Crown Hill Cemetery. To see the grand 1885 Gothic Gate, enter at the intersection of 34th Street and Boulevard Place.

JAMES WHITCOMB RILEY

James Whitcomb Riley is known as the "Hoosier Poet" and is most famous for his poem "Little Orphant Annie." Riley is buried in Crown Hill Cemetery, and two museums in Indiana celebrate his life and legacy.

James Whitcomb Riley Boyhood Home & Museum
250 W Main St., Greenfield, (317) 462-8539
jwrileyhome.org

James Whitcomb Riley Museum Home
528 Lockerbie St., Indianapolis, (317) 631-5885
rileymuseumhome.org

The Riley Festival
Indiana's largest four-day festival celebrating the birth date of James Whitcomb Riley every October.
Greenfield, (317) 462-2141
rileyfestival.com

TOUR
THE KOKOMO OPALESCENT GLASS FACTORY

You can walk through the oldest hand-cast, cathedral, and opalescent glass company in America and experience blown-glass demonstrations at Kokomo Opalescent Glass (KOG). The same techniques for making glass in 1888 are used today: the glass is hand-ladled, rolled from a furnace, and blown into artistic masterpieces.

Tiffany was one of the most prominent and largest customers of KOG until the 1890s. Glass produced by KOG can be found around the world. Locations include the Vatican, Disney World, and the White House, to name a few. Tours of the factory are offered three days a week and need to be scheduled in advance. Visitors must wear closed-toed, thick-soled shoes. Everyone on the tour gets to take home a complimentary gift.

1310 S Market St., Kokomo, (765) 457-1829
kog.com

TIP

Explore beyond Kokomo and challenge yourself to the Indiana Glass Trail. The trail covers studios, museums, blown-glass demonstrations, festivals, and classes in five counties. indianaglasstrail.com

COME ABOARD

THE USS *LST-325*

The USS *LST-325* was used during WWII and decommissioned in 1946. In 2001, the ship was brought to Evansville, where it is docked for 11 months of the year and used for cruises for one month each summer. It is the last surviving fully functioning LST in the country. Guided tours of the ship last an hour. The ship is docked on the Ohio River and exposed to the elements, so dress accordingly. Comfortable walking shoes are recommended. A shorter accessible tour is available for those who need to avoid stairs. Start your visit at the USS *LST* Ship Memorial's visitor center.

Tours begin every hour; the last one of the day begins at three in the afternoon. Pictures and questions during tours are welcomed.

610 NW Riverside Dr., Evansville, (812) 435-8678
lstmemorial.org

TIP

Admission is free for active military members and first responders.

74

ENCOUNTER THE LIFE OF A HOLLYWOOD LEGEND

AT THE JAMES DEAN GALLERY

James Dean was a cool, young, 1950s heartthrob when he became a Hollywood actor and legend. Dean grew up in Fairmount and was an avid auto racer. He dreamed of one day racing in the Indianapolis 500. His dream was cut short, however, when an automobile accident took his life at the age of 24. Today you can visit the James Dean Gallery in his hometown, filled with thousands of pieces of memorabilia, an art display, a screening room, a library, and collectibles. The gallery is in a restored 1903 Victorian home and was opened in 1988. An antique shop called Rebel Rebel is located in the back of the museum.

The gallery is open daily and is free to visit. Don't forget to snap a photo with the James Dean statue in front of the museum!

425 N Main St., Fairmount, (765) 948-3326
jamesdeangallery.com

JAMES DEAN LANDMARKS TRAIL

(765) 668-5435
showmegrantcounty.com/grant-county-attractions/
james-dean

Fairmount Historical Museum
The world's largest collection
of Dean's personal belongings.
203 E Washington St., Fairmount, (765) 948-4555
jamesdeanartifacts.com

James Dean Birthsite Memorial
The site of the House of Seven Gables, the home
where Dean was born.
410 S McClure St., Marion

James Dean Memorial Park
A green space and memorial dedicated to Dean.
200 N Main St., Fairmount

Park Cemetery
Dean's final resting place.
8008 S 150 E, Fairmount, (765) 948-4040

75

SEE THE EARTHEN MOUNDS
AT ANGEL MOUNDS STATE HISTORIC SITE

More than a thousand people from the Mississippian culture once resided at the Angel Mounds State Historic Site. This area served as more than just a ceremonial site; it was a community with homes and shops. It is the best preserved pre-contact Native American site in the country. It includes more than 600 acres: 103 acres of a town that was built between AD 1000 and 1450 and 500 acres dedicated to a nature preserve, trails, and an 18-hole disc golf course.

Start your visit at the interpretive center and then take a hike around the 12 earthen mounds. The Angel Mounds Loop Trail is a mostly flat four-mile trail that is great for families.

8215 Pollack Ave., Evansville, (812) 853-3956
indianamuseum.org/historic-sites/angel-mounds

TIP

Explore the Eiteljorg Museum of American Indians and Western Art in downtown Indianapolis to learn more about the indigenous peoples of North America. 500 W Washington St., Indianapolis, (317) 636-9378
eiteljorg.org

NATIVE AMERICAN MOUND SITES

Mounds State Park
4306 Mounds Rd., Anderson, (765) 642-6627
on.in.gov/moundssp

Strawtown Koteewi Park
12302 E Strawtown Ave., Noblesville, (317) 774-2574
hamiltoncounty.in.gov/facilities/facility/details/
strawtown-koteewi-park-11

Sugar Loaf Mound
2425 Wabash Ave., Vincennes, (812) 703-4004

RELAX, REFLECT, OR PRAY
AT SAINT MARY-OF-THE-WOODS

Saint Mary-of-the-Woods, also called the Woods, is a Catholic community run by the Sisters of Providence. The Woods is a beautiful, peaceful, and historic campus. It is open for the public to tour, hike or bike the campus trails, shop at Linden Leaf Gifts or the Farm Store at the White Violet Center, enjoy Sunday brunch, or visit the alpaca farm. Admission is free, except for private tours of the alpaca farm. The campus is open seven days a week for self-guided tours, but guided tours must be scheduled in advance.

Start your tour at the Shrine of Saint Mother Theodore Guerin (it's also a museum); enter through the entrance of the Providence Spirituality & Conference Center. Then explore the rest of the campus, which includes a remarkable church, several chapels, and a grotto. The Woods is listed on the National Register of Historic Places.

1 Sisters of Providence, Saint Mary-of-the-Woods, (812) 535-3131
spsmw.org/visit

TOUR SACRED AND HISTORIC PLACES

Basilica of the Sacred Heart & Grotto of Our Lady of Lourdes
University of Notre Dame
101 Basilica Dr., Notre Dame, (574) 631-9050
campusministry.nd.edu/mass-worship/basilica-of-the-sacred-heart

Monastery Immaculate Conception
802 E 10th St., Ferdinand, (812) 367-1411
thedome.org/at-the-monastery/visit-the-monastery

Old Cathedral Catholic Church (Basilica of St. Francis Xavier)
205 Church St., Vincennes, (812) 882-5638
stfrancisxaviervincennes.com

Saint Meinrad Archabbey
200 Hill Dr., St. Meinrad, (812) 357-6611
saintmeinrad.org/visit-us

77

VISIT A LIVING HISTORY MUSEUM
AT CONNER PRAIRIE

Step back in time at Indiana's outdoor living history museum with a visit to Conner Prairie. Its 1836 Prairietown, 1863 Civil War Journey, and Lenape Indian Camp exhibits enable guests to immerse themselves in the experience, learn, see presentations, and interact with the actors. It truly is a one-of-a-kind encounter for both children and adults. For younger children, there are hands-on experiences like water play areas and the indoor Discovery Station.

At Animal Encounters, you can get up close to the farm animals, chat with the caretakers, and pet the goats. The Treetop Outpost is a kid favorite. It's a four-story treehouse made for climbing, playing, and exploring. A 1.2-mile nature trail has a view of the restored prairie next to the treehouse.

13400 Allisonville Rd., Fishers, (317) 776-6000
connerprairie.org

TIP

If you have little ones, you can grab an Adventure Backpack at the Welcome Center with tools and toys for them to use on your visit.

SIGHTSEE
ON THE INDIANA LIMESTONE HERITAGE TRAIL

Monroe and Lawrence counties are well known for their limestone contributions to iconic buildings around the nation. The Empire State Building, Pentagon, and Lincoln Memorial are just a few of the many buildings built using limestone from Monroe County's Salem Limestone quarry. Indiana's incredible limestone will be enjoyed for centuries because of the beauty created by architects and artists around the world.

Take the Indiana Limestone Heritage Trail to see some of these creations. The self-guided driving trail will take you to sculptures, museums, state parks, restaurants, and other limestone sites. Please note that quarries are on private property. Do not try to access these quarries unless you are on a scheduled tour.

limestonemonth.com

TIP

For a self-guided tour of the Limestone Trail, you can download a map online. Pack a picnic to enjoy at one of the scenic stops, or grab a bite to eat at one of the restaurants on the trail.

VIEW A MUMMY
AT THE WAYNE COUNTY HISTORICAL MUSEUM

There are only two places you can see a real mummy in Indiana, and both of those places are in Richmond. The Wayne County Historical Museum's founder, Julia Meek Gaar, was a world traveler and donated her extensive collection to the museum. The museum is located in the former Friends Meeting House, which is listed on the National Register of Historic Places. Among the items in the collection is a 3,000-year-old mummy that Gaar purchased in Cairo, Egypt, in 1929.

Outside there is a replica of Richmond in the 1800s that you can walk through. Inside the museum are two levels of exhibits. My favorite is the mock Main Street of Richmond's early days (found on the lower level). It's an impressive collection for a small-town county museum.

1150 N A St., Richmond, (765) 962-5756
wchmuseum.org

TIP

The second mummy can be found at the Joseph Moore Museum, located on the Earlham College campus. 801 National Rd. W, Richmond, (765) 983-1303, jmm.earlham.edu

WALK THROUGH THE UNDERGROUND RUINS OF THE CATACOMBS

Did you know there are hidden passageways underneath City Market, the oldest farmers' market in Indianapolis? A solo staircase leads to 20,000 square feet of brick archways, limestone walls, and dirt floors. Indiana Landmarks calls this underground space the Catacombs.

The Catacombs are also underneath the former Tomlinson Hall, which was next to City Market but burned down in 1958. But the musty and damp underground world remains. There is not much to see except what appears to be endless brickwork, but the history is fascinating, and the tour is even a bit creepy for those intrigued by eerie tales. Indiana Landmarks offers guided tours on select days every month and after-hour tours for adults only.

222 E Market St., Indianapolis, (317) 639-4534
indianalandmarks.org/tours-events/ongoing-tours-events/city-market-catacombs-tour

Warm Glow Candle Company

SHOPPING AND FASHION

STROLL THROUGH
THE QUAINT VILLAGE OF NASHVILLE

Unlike its Tennessee namesake, life slows down in Nashville, Indiana. Nashville is the county seat for Brown County, known as the "Art Colony of the Midwest." It's a quaint village composed of boutiques, antique shops, cafés, gift shops, art studios, and galleries. Strolls through downtown lead to shops full of crafts, artwork, and treats. You can also dine at unique restaurants and breweries, all at your own pace.

Stay for a weekend at a bed and breakfast, inn, or Airbnb in the village. There are plenty of things to do to fill a vacation in Nashville. Fall is a very busy season for Brown County, so you'll want to make reservations in advance. Visit the Brown County Visitors Center for a map of the village; it's located in the heart of downtown.

Brown County Visitors Center
211 S Van Buren St., Nashville, (812) 988-7303
browncounty.com/shop

TIP

While in Nashville, visit Brown County State Park. It's a scenic hot spot in the fall.

FIND YOUR FAVORITE FRAGRANCE
AT THE WARM GLOW CANDLE STORE

Have you seen the world's largest candle? It's 80 feet tall and located at the Warm Glow Candle Store—home to candles in more than 70 different fragrances. That is a lot of scent options! The store is directly off of I-70 in Centerville, and the world's largest candle makes it hard to miss. Warm Glow candles are all hand-dipped in Indiana and have a signature "lumpy bumpy" look. The best-selling Hearth Candles weigh two pounds and burn for up to 150 hours—they are enormous!

In addition to candles, the store is full of home decor, accessories, local artisan booths, crafts, chocolates, wine, and gifts. A café inside sells food, drinks, and desserts, and there is a coffee shop.

2131 N Centerville Rd., Centerville, (765) 855-2000
warmglow.com

TIP

The shop has large events every spring, fall, and winter to welcome in the season with new inventory.

83

DILLYDALLY
AROUND DAVIS MERCANTILE

At Davis Mercantile you can shop, play, eat, gather, and relax. Located just around the corner from the Blue Gate Theatre, Davis Mercantile is a must for anyone visiting Shipshewana. It's the most unique shop in town, with four floors and over 20 shops in one building. It's particularly special because of the 1906 Dentzel Carousel located on the top floor. Each of the carousel animals was hand-carved to represent animals you'd see around Shipshewana. You can even take a ride on the carousel.

The shops at Davis Mercantile stock clothing and accessories, home decor, furniture, musical instruments, toys and puzzles, fabrics, candy, and more. There's also a coffee shop and café. The Mercantile is open six days a week, but keep in mind it is closed on Sundays (like much of Shipshewana).

225 N Harrison St., Shipshewana, (260) 768-7300
davismercantile.com

TIP

The Shipshewana Flea Market takes place May to September. It's a very busy season in Shipshewana, so keep this in mind if you are planning to make local reservations.

BROWSE THROUGH
THE HISTORIC COPPES COMMONS

The Coppes Bros. Box Factory and Planing Mill produced kitchen cabinets ("Hoosier cabinets") and furniture from 1883 until the 1990s. In 2007, the building went through a major renovation to become Coppes Commons, a community of small businesses with shops, restaurants, an event center, and the Hoosier Cabinet Museum. It is Nappanee's most historic site.

The shops include a bookstore, boutique, antique shop, toy store, bakery, and gift shop, as well as food vendors selling popcorn, pretzels, and ice cream. Rocket Science makes ice cream with liquid nitrogen and also sells treats like bubble tea. The Country Home Shoppe sells locally made Amish quilts and giftware.

401 E Market St., Nappanee, (574) 773-0002
coppescommons.com

TIP

The Barns at Nappanee is a popular place to explore Amish heritage. Dine on homestyle comfort foods and catch a performance in the round-barn theater. 1600 W Market St., Nappanee, (574) 773-4188
thebarnsatnappanee.com

85

HUNT FOR TREASURES AND TRINKETS
IN ANTIQUE ALLEY

Cambridge City is in the heart of Indiana's Antique Alley, the largest network of antique stores in the Midwest. Within two blocks, there are more than 10 antique shops, including the National Road Antique Mall. Down the road is the 83,000-square-foot Centerville Antique Mall. Along the Historic National Road (US 40) in East Central Indiana are small towns filled with antique shops and antique malls. These towns include Dunreith, Dublin, East Germantown, Farmland, Hagerstown, Knightstown, Lewisville, Lynn, New Castle, Redkey, Richmond, and Winchester.

Antique Alley is a 66-mile loop and is divided into two trails; you can spend quite a bit of time hunting for treasures here.

visitrichmond.org/visitors/things-to-do/antique-alley

TIP

The Historic National Road Yard Sale takes place annually on the Wednesday through Sunday after Memorial Day. It spans the entire state along the Historic National Road (US 40).
facebook.com/nationalroadyardsaleUS40

86

SHOP AND SIP
AT URBAN FARMCHIC

If you mix modern fashion with home goods, put them in a historic 1850s hotel building, and add a coffee bar, you'll get Urban Farmchic in downtown Rockville. That is what makes this boutique and coffee shop so unique. It has a little bit of everything, for everyone: women, men, children, and even pets. The storefront lined with antiques is inviting and pulls you in for a peek. Inside, visitors are welcomed with the smell of coffee and sweet treats. The coffee bar serves lunch, bakery items, coffee, and bubble teas.

The boutique takes over the rest of the store with home goods, fashion, industrial finds, and gifts. Vintage, handmade, and salvage items are also for sale throughout the store. If you find a fashionable item you'd like to try on, you can step into the dressing room made out of a truck cab.

102 S Market St., Rockville, (765) 245-2015
facebook.com/urbanfarmchic

SNAG A DEAL
AT THE VERA BRADLEY ANNUAL OUTLET SALE

Colorful, bold, bright, and fun quilted Vera Bradley bags and accessories have made quite the worldwide name for themselves since the 1990s. Fort Wayne is headquarters for Vera Bradley, and every year the company puts on a huge outlet sale. It's not just any discount sale. People come from all over the country for the five-day sale that draws in more than 50,000 visitors every spring. They're all hoping to get their hands on heavily discounted handbags, luggage, wallets, and accessories.

The sale is held at the Allen County War Memorial Coliseum. There are over 100,000 square feet of space with tables of discounted items. Guests can purchase time-slotted tickets in advance for the first three days; the last two days are free to attend. Items are sold first-come, first-served.

(888) 855-8372
verabradley.com/pages/annual-outlet-sale

TIP

For overnight accommodations, check out The Bradley, a Vera Bradley-owned and themed hotel in downtown Fort Wayne. 204 W Main St., Fort Wayne, (260) 428-4018, provenancehotels.com/the-bradley

LOOK FOR BARGAINS
AT THE INDIANA PREMIUM OUTLETS

Often referred to as the "Edinburgh Outlets," the Indiana Premium Outlets are located 30 miles south of Indianapolis just off of Interstate 65. Unlike most malls, this outdoor shopping plaza is located in a small town. And it's the biggest outlet mall in the state. Bargain hunters travel here to find name brands such as Coach, Kate Spade New York, Michael Kors, Nike, Polo Ralph Lauren, and Vera Bradley at steep discounts. There are more than 70 stores to shop from.

Stop by Big Woods or the Food Truck Plaza to refuel during your shopping spree. Have fun shopping till you drop!

11622 NE Executive Dr., Edinburgh, (812) 526-9764
premiumoutlets.com/outlet/indiana

TIP

Lighthouse Place Premium Outlets is another outdoor shopping mall. This one is located in northwest Indiana, less than a mile from Lake Michigan in Michigan City. 601 Wabash St., Michigan City, (219) 879-6506
premiumoutlets.com/outlet/lighthouse-place

89

TRAVEL THROUGH TIME
AT WHO NORTH AMERICA

The popular British sci-fi series *Doctor Who* is well known in Camby—home to the only *Doctor Who* retail store and museum in the United States. As you walk into Who North America, you'll first notice a life-sized TARDIS. It's a popular photo spot in Hendricks County and should be on the bucket list of every Whovian (fan of the show). On one side of the building is the retail store, and on the other is the Museum of Merchandise.

Shelves upon shelves of *Doctor Who* books, comics, action figures, clothing, mugs, costumes, movies, jewelry, household items, and more are available in the retail section. There is a little bit of everything. The museum showcases more than 50 years of merchandise and special pieces. It is always free to visit.

8901 S State Rd. 67, Camby, (317) 481-8189
whona.com

BUY JUMBO JELLY BEANS
AT THE WAKARUSA DIME STORE

In 1969, the Wakarusa Dime Store was given the task of creating a new candy for the Maple Syrup Festival. Lou Wolfberg created jumbo jelly beans, and they were a hit! The candy became world-famous and can be found only at the Wakarusa Dime Store. The store sells more than 75 tons of jelly beans annually, in more than 15 flavors. The chocolate-covered cherry and tangy fruit assortment are two of my favorites. The store carries a variety of other candies, as well. There are more than 450 kinds, from old-fashioned favorites to weird and unusual candy treats. There is a little bit of something for everyone!

103 E Waterford St., Wakarusa, (574) 862-4690
jumbojellybeans.com

TIP

Wakarusa Dime Store has a second location in Granger, and you can purchase the jumbo jelly beans online as well. 340 W Cleveland Rd., Granger, (574) 855-4473

Ann Dancing on Massachusetts Avenue

MAIN STREETS AND NEIGHBORHOODS

ADMIRE THE HOMES
IN THE MADISON HISTORIC DISTRICT

Downtown Madison has more than 130 blocks of historic homes and amazing architecture. There are eight house museums, the History Center, and three National Historic Landmarks, including the Lanier Mansion State Historic Site. It is the largest contiguous National Historic Landmark District in the country.

The bluffs of the Ohio River offer a picturesque background for the spirited Main Street. The downtown area offers restaurants, cafés, boutiques, antique shops, and inns. Drive through to see the streets lined with historic homes or take a self-guided walking tour.

sites.google.com/view/historicmadisoninc

Lanier Mansion State Historic Site
601 W 1st St., Madison, (812) 265-3526
indianamuseum.org/historic-sites/lanier-mansion

TIP

Visit Clifty Falls State Park in Madison for outdoor recreation, including hiking, picnicking, playgrounds, camping, and scenic views of waterfalls and canyons. 2221 Clifty Dr., Madison, (812) 273-8885
on.in.gov/cliftyfallssp

LINGER A LITTLE LONGER
IN THE VILLAGE AT WINONA

Indiana may not have an ocean, but it has the beautiful Winona Lake. The Village at Winona is a community of homes, restaurants, shops, trails, parks, and inns surrounded by the lake. Throughout the year it's a destination, and the calendar is filled with events and activities such as Canal Days.

The village has always been a place for community. In 1887, the area was purchased and turned into a resort by two dairy farmers. They then sold the resort to a church leader, who added more buildings, cottages, and a canal to repurpose the resort into a retreat center. For years, the village flourished as a religious haven. A restoration project in the 1990s breathed new life into the village. Now it is a place for both residents and visitors to eat, play, and stay.

700 Park Ave., Winona Lake, (574) 268-9888
villageatwinona.com

POSE WITH PUBLIC ART
IN THE CARMEL ARTS & DESIGN DISTRICT

Have your camera ready when you visit the Carmel Arts & Design District. You'll find plenty of opportunities to snap photos in Indiana's premier location for art. The district is home to more than 100 art and design businesses, such as shops and boutiques selling paintings, handicrafts, pottery, jewelry, and more. If you are looking for an architect, art gallery, studio, or interior designer, you will find one here as well.

Main Street and the surrounding blocks are lined with public art from the Carmel Public Art Collection. More than 15 life-sized "Man-on-the-Street" series sculptures can be found in the area. Have a seat next to the businessman sculpture in front of the ArtSplash Gallery or wave to the police officer statue in front of Bub's Burgers (and challenge yourself to the "Big Ugly" burger while you are there).

30 W Main St., Ste. 220, Carmel, (317) 571-ARTS
carmelartsanddesign.com

CHECK OUT WHERE FORT WAYNE BEGAN
AT THE LANDING

Before Fort Wayne became a city, the Landing was the already a hot spot in the area. This historic neighborhood is home to Fort Wayne's first county meetings and courts, and the first post office and hotel. It's been preserved and restored as one of the admired hangouts in the city. The Landing is a vibrant neighborhood of restaurants, apartments, businesses, coffee shops, and a hotel. It is surrounded by theaters, gardens, parks, and event centers. Across the street, Promenade Park is a popular spot for residents and guests to enjoy.

Events throughout the year bring in food trucks, entertainers, and live music. The surrounding downtown blocks are known as the "neighborhood" and offer out-of-towners places to stay overnight and additional activities to explore.

thelandingfw.com

TIP

Check out the murals. The Landing has several that are on Fort Wayne's Public Art Trail. visitfortwayne.com/publicarttrail

CUT A RUG WITH *ANN DANCING* ON MASSACHUSETTS AVENUE

What is there to do in Indianapolis? Lots of things! A local might tell you to "check out Mass Ave." The Mass Ave Cultural Arts District is a popular community known for its diagonal street. The five blocks of Mass Ave include Italianate commercial buildings, historic homes, restaurants, shops, and entertainment venues. Popular historic buildings such as the Athenaeum, Murat, and Coca-Cola bottling plant are located in this district.

Arts and theatre are a huge part of Mass Ave. Step into the Chatterbox Jazz Club for live music or find *Ann Dancing*, the large LED display of an animated woman dancing. The night is always young for those interested in the food and entertainment scene on Mass Ave.

massavelydifferent.com

TIP

Broad Ripple is another popular neighborhood near downtown Indianapolis, but it has more of a neighborhood feel. The Indianapolis Art Center, a farmer's market, cafés, shops, and other small businesses line the village. broadrippleindy.org

THE BOTTLEWORKS DISTRICT ON MASS AVE.

The Bottleworks District is located within the Mass Ave Cultural Arts District. In 2017 the old Coca-Cola bottling plant was repurposed as an entertainment destination, with a movie theater, a massive food hall, a hotel, and a duckpin bowling facility.

Bottleworks Hotel
850 Massachusetts Ave., Indianapolis, (317) 556-1234
bottleworkshotel.com

The Garage Food Hall
906 Carrollton Ave., Indianapolis, (317) 556-1252
garageindy.com

PRESERVE THE PAST
IN THE IRVINGTON HISTORIC DISTRICT

Indianapolis's first suburb, Irvington, is now the city's largest protected historic district. It is located along the Historic National Road (US 40), so it makes a great stop for those traveling the popular route. The Irvington Historic District consists of over 2,800 buildings, the majority of which were built from the late 1800s to 1960. Stroll through Irvington to find pizza, a tiki bar, gift shops, coffee, ice cream, trails, a farmers' market, and other shops.

The district was named after Washington Irving, the author of "The Legend of Sleepy Hollow." Irvington is most famous for its Halloween Festival, the biggest Halloween party in Indiana, where the Headless Horseman often makes an appearance. People come from all over for the ghost tours, parade, Night Out in Sleepy Hollow, street fair, and more.

irvingtoncommunitycouncil.com

TREK BACK IN TIME
TO THE HISTORIC VILLAGE OF METAMORA

Metamora is known as "Indiana's canal town" because it was the industrial hub for trading along the Whitewater Canal in the 1830s and 1840s. It's one of the oldest communities in Indiana and is listed on the National Register of Historic Places. The village is small and located in the middle of nowhere, but people travel from all over to visit Metamora, especially over the holidays and during its biggest event of the year, Canal Days. The Whitewater Valley Railroad offers passengers a scenic ride to Metamora from Connersville every weekend.

The Whitewater Canal is the only functioning canal left in Indiana. The Whitewater Canal State Historic Site is situated on the canal and has an operating grist mill, which has been using water to mill corn for over 100 years. Visit the site along with over 30 shops, restaurants, inns, and more.

historicmetamora.net

Whitewater Canal State Historic Site
19073 Main St., Metamora, (765) 647-6512
indianamuseum.org/historic-sites/white-water-canal

SLIP AWAY TO A UTOPIAN COMMUNITY IN NEW HARMONY

In the early 1800s, two utopian communities settled in New Harmony. The first was a religious community called the Rappites; it was then sold to a second community, the Owenites, who were mostly important scholars. By 1827 the utopian community had moved on, but the buildings remained. The preservation of New Harmony has kept its legacy alive.

Start your visit to New Harmony with a visit to the Atheneum Visitors Center; take a tour of the historic sites, homes, and theaters; and walk through the hedges of the Harmonist Labyrinth. Just do a bit of wandering through town, and you'll discover why New Harmony has a likable and alluring charm.

401 N Arthur St., New Harmony, (812) 682-3702
indianamuseum.org/historic-sites/new-harmony

TIP

Visit Harmonie State Park for its walking, biking, mountain biking, and nature trails. 3451 Harmonie State Park Rd., New Harmony (812) 682-4821, on.in.gov/harmoniesp

SPEND A DAY
IN DOWNTOWN BLOOMINGTON

Bloomington (also referred to as “B-Town”) has a lively downtown community. The courthouse square is home to over 30 local businesses and restaurants surrounding the Monroe County Courthouse. During the holidays, the square is lit up with the Canopy of Lights, and downtown looks like a scene from a holiday movie. Restaurant options are ample, including international options, coffee shops, and late-night foodie fare. The after-dinner crowd will enjoy the plethora of music venues and entertainment, such as a comedy club and arcade bars.

During the day, browse the shops and boutiques. You’ll even find unique gems like a teahouse, comic book shop, vintage tee and sneaker shop, bookstores, and a rock-and-roll themed pizza joint. The downtown Bloomington community welcomes visitors day and night.

downtownbloomington.com

TIP

Street parking can be difficult to find on nights and weekends, but there are affordable parking garages. Metered parking and parking garages are free on Sundays.

100

HEAD TO THE ARCHITECTURE DESTINATION OF THE MIDWEST

IN DOWNTOWN COLUMBUS

Although Columbus is a small city, it's a world-famous architectural mecca. There isn't a block in Columbus without significant art or architecture. The American Institute of Architects has ranked Columbus alongside big cities such as Chicago and New York for its architectural innovation and design.

Start your visit at the Columbus Area Visitors Center. It offers guided architectural tours, and tickets can be reserved in advance on the website. Alternatively, you can download a map for a free self-guided tour. Fifth Street is known as the "Avenue of the Architects" and highlights some of the most popular buildings. It is walkable in the warmer months.

Columbus Area Visitors Center
506 5th St., Columbus, (812) 378-2622
columbus.in.us/guide-to-the-architecture

DID YOU KNOW?

Families with children up to 12 years old will love the Commons Playground in downtown Columbus. It's a 5,000-square-foot indoor playground that was created by artist Thomas Luckey, and it's free to visit.

300 Washington St., Columbus, (812) 376-2681
thecommonscolumbus.com/james-a-henderson-playground

ACTIVITIES
BY SEASON

SPRING

SUMMER

FALL

WINTER

SUGGESTED ITINERARIES

DATE NIGHT

FOR YOUNGER CHILDREN

FOR TEENS

GIRLS' GETAWAYS

UNIQUE AND UNUSUAL

OUTDOOR EXPLORING

FREE THINGS TO DO

REST AND RELAX

TAKE A CHALLENGE

ICONIC INDIANA

INDEX